KT-154-298

Heal The Sick

Heal The Sick

REGINALD EAST

HODDER AND STOUGHTON
LONDON SYDNEY AUCKLAND TORONTO

Copyright © 1977 by Reginald East. First printed 1977.
ISBN 0 340 21669 7. All rights reserved. No part of this publication
may be reproduced or transmitted in any form or by any means,
electronic or mechanical, including photocopy, recording, or any
information storage and retrieval system, without permission in
writing from the publisher. This book is sold subject to the condition
that it shall not, by way of trade or otherwise, be lent, re-sold, hired
out or otherwise circulated without the publisher's prior consent in any
form of binding or cover other than that in which this is published
and without a similar condition including this condition being imposed
on the subsequent purchaser. Printed in Great Britain for Hodder and
Stoughton Limited, Mill Road, Dunton Green, Sevenoaks, Kent, by
C. Nicholls & Company Ltd, The Philips Park Press, Manchester.

Contents

To my wife

*Together, by God's grace, we found the healing
Christ to offer to others.*

*'For I will restore health to you and your
wounds
I will heal, says the Lord'* (*Jer. 39:17*).

Foreword

THE AIM OF this book is to encourage Christians, ordained and lay, in local churches to take the healing ministry 'into their system'. To this end I have presented the healing ministry in a practical way so that those who have had little or no previous experience of the ministry may feel themselves able to take their part in it. In this province of the Church's mission, 'The harvest is plentiful, but the labourers are few; pray therefore the Lord of the harvest to send out labourers into his harvest' (Matt.9:37–8).

Although as a priest of the Church of England I have been influenced by what is called the Charismatic Renewal, it is my hope that what has been written will be of use to Christians of all traditions.

Since a human being is a unity of body, mind and spirit – which closely react upon each other – I have given some attention to physical as well as to emotional and spiritual healing. The first three chapters are concerned with the healing ministry generally. Chapters four and five refer especially to healing of physical complaints, while chapters seven onwards are devoted to emotional and spiritual illnesses. At the end of the book there is a short appendix on the deliverance ministry.

I would express my gratitude to the community to which I belong for their encouragement in the writing of this book, for making it possible for time to be given to it, and for helping both by suggestions and in the typing of the manuscript. Particularly am I indebted to the Rev. John Gunstone, formerly chaplain of this community, for his invaluable help and constructive criticism.

WHATCOMBE HOUSE,   REGINALD EAST
WINTERBORNE WHITECHURCH,
BLANDFORD, DORSET

I

Healing is wholeness

Not many months after becoming a curate, a member of the youth club of my church asked me to lay hands on a baby who had a brain tumour. My first reaction was one of panic. I telephoned the only person I knew who had experience of the healing ministry, and his quiet reply was 'Go and lay hands on the child.' Never have I experienced such a miserable journey! I had little or no faith that anything would happen if I prayed for the child and so I felt I was going to that home under false pretences. I have no recollection of what I said to the young couple before praying for their baby, and I left them feeling that I had let them down badly. The baby died soon afterwards.

This experience made me feel a failure. It also caused me to question whether the healing of the sick was part of the ministry of the Church. Not long afterwards, when visiting a sick person, I laid hands on her. As I went through the bedroom door on my way out I glanced back to the lady in bed and saw, to my astonishment, that her face had a new light and joy in it. I realised then that in the act of laying on of hands God had given her grace. This encouraged me to continue to pray and lay hands on people for a variety of needs, and as time went on it became clear to me that healing was part of the Church's ministry. Slowly I gained confidence in offering to pray with people, and was content to leave the outcome with our Lord.

The big obstacle I had to overcome was fear. The question haunted me: 'Suppose nothing happens when I lay hands on someone who is ill? Shall I feel that I have let them down? Surely they will be disappointed and so I will only have added to their suffering!' This fear needs to be faced by all who are called to this ministry. It has power over us because it is fixed in our inadequacy and weakness of faith. To counteract these we must be always 'looking to Jesus the pioneer and perfecter of our faith' (Heb.12:2) for it is at His command that we minister and it is His power which heals. So, in my own case, I had to trust in these two things as best I could and persist in the ministry. At times God helped me to overcome my reluctance by bringing me face to face with sick people who needed and who sometimes asked for ministry.

When we step out in faith to pray for someone who is ill, it often happens that we do not see immediately the result for which we ask. When this is the case, we need not imagine that we have failed the sick person and God. If we do, we may be deterred from again praying with the sick. I have learnt, as have others who practise this ministry, that we must not determine beforehand what Christ will do. It is common experience that healing can be for some reason delayed. Nothing is seen to happen at the time we pray to suggest that healing has been received, but later the sick person realises that it is taking place. It is also likely that healing may be delayed because our Lord has to do a preliminary work of dealing with an underlying obstacle such as lack of faith, a sin, or an emotional disorder.

We must remember that healing, in the Christian sense, means healing of the whole person. When we minister healing in Christ's name, we minister the whole of His redemptive love to the whole of a person's being. Our

Lord's redeeming work was to free humanity from the total effect of sin, evil and ignorance. This realisation, again, helped me to lose my fear of ministering to sick people, and as I entered into the ministry so I saw the grace of God at work on body, mind and spirit.

Christ's healing ministry

As I was drawn more and more into it, I became aware of a new interest in our Lord's own healing work. At first I studied the instances of physical healing in the Gospels, but later I saw how all embracing His ministry was.

I noticed Jesus indicated that His work for us was one whole when He used the same word meaning 'to save' for both the salvation of the soul as well as for the healing of the body. In Zacchaeus's house after the dramatic change in Zacchaeus He said, 'Today salvation has come to this house ... For the Son of man came to seek and to save the lost' (Luke 19:9–10). Jesus used the same word to the blind man at Jericho when He sealed His healing action with the words, 'Receive your sight, your faith has saved you' (R.S.V. 'made you whole') (Luke 18:42).

Our Lord set this pattern of His ministry at the outset when He took to Himself the words of Isaiah:

> The Spirit of the Lord is upon me,
> because he has anointed me to preach good news to the
>   poor,
> He sent me to proclaim release to the captives
> and recovery of sight to the blind,
> to set at liberty those who are oppressed,
> to proclaim the acceptable year of the Lord.
>   (Luke 4:18–19)

This proclamation covers God's care for spirit, mind and body.

Jesus went on to demonstrate the inclusiveness of this ministry by preaching and teaching, casting out demons and healing the sick (Luke 4:31-41). Such a comprehensive form of ministry was realised by Matthew when in one of the summaries he gives of our Lord's work he referred directly to Isaiah 53:3-5, 'That evening they brought to him many that were possessed with demons; and he cast out the spirits with a word, and healed all who were sick. This was to fulfil what was spoken by the prophet Isaiah, He took our infirmities and bore our diseases' (Matt. 8:16-17).

This is the nature of the healing ministry as the Gospels present it. It covers more than the healing of the body, but to exclude that would mean we are not fully expressing the ministry Christ had given to His Church. Jesus's own ministry so abounds with physical healings that to eliminate them would change the whole tenor of it. It is no surprise, therefore, that He should say to John the Baptist that these healings, with the preaching of the good news, were the evidence that He was the One who was to come (Matt. 11:2-5). They must still be the evidence of His salvation.

What compassion must have flowed from our Lord's heart as He looked around at the sea of faces, each with its own need! We can feel the ache in His heart as He saw them as 'sheep without a shepherd' and said to His disciples, 'The harvest is plentiful, but the labourers are few' (Matt. 9:37). He therefore trained His disciples to share this ministry. We have glimpses of this training in the missions of the twelve and of the seventy, and also when He took Peter, James and John with Him when He healed Jairus's daughter. His words to the disciples on a later occasion when they were unable to heal the boy with the dumb spirit are significant, 'O faithless generation, how long am I to be with you? How long am I to bear with you: Bring him to me' (Mark 9:19). These words would appear to mean that by now He expected them to be able to deal with such a situation, and they express His strong disappointment. The same need both for healing and for training to bring it about is no less today.

Christ's physical healings covered a wide range of suffering. Matthew records that He healed 'every disease and every infirmity' and he specifies 'pains, demons, epileptics and paralytics' (4:23-24), but more of the then unrecognised conditions must also have been cured. If we add leprosy, blindness, deafness, dumbness and cripples through disease and accident, it is clear that few, if any, physical needs were not met by Jesus.

It would appear from the Gospels that our Lord did not approach people with the offer to heal. They seem always to have come to Him. It was those who came who were healed. It may be that our Lord so acted in order to test faith as well as to discourage the establishing of a reputation as a wonder worker.

The gifts of the Spirit are also evident in His ministry. The gift of faith is apparent, among other instances, in the healing of Peter's mother-in-law, since it was at the very commencement of His ministry and so unlikely that her faith in Him would have reached a high level. Jesus must, therefore, by the gift of faith, have known that she would be healed. Other gifts also are seen. Discernment of spirits is evident in His dealings with evil spirits. The word of knowledge was given to Him on various occasions. In the healing of Jairus's daughter, when the messenger announced the child's death, Jesus said, 'Do not fear, only believe.' He knew the child would recover and went on to announce in a word of knowledge, 'The child is not dead but sleeping'

(Mark 5:39). At the healing of the man borne by four friends by a word of knowledge Jesus realised that the sick man's need was for forgiveness before physical healing (Mark 2:5).

While we have mainly in the Gospels accounts of physical healings, there are enough instances of His dealings with 'damaged' people to point to the full extent of His caring. His teaching in itself must have healed much inner suffering and shown many the way out of their ghettos of hurt and inner pain. It would also have drawn some with compulsive force to find a release at His hands. When they came to Him they found Someone who not only understood perfectly their need, but who also identified Himself with it.

Such a person was the woman who came to Him in Simon the Pharisee's house when they were at dinner (Luke 7:36ff). Jesus took her part against Simon and accepted her, and her tears, her kiss, her ointment. His forgiveness and acceptance, which drew out her love for Him ('she loved much'), released her from her dissolute past and gave her a new beginning. The same release from the past was given to the woman taken in adultery (John 8:2ff.). He shared her humiliation, her need to be loved which she had tried to satisfy wrongly, and her dread of being stoned to death. Having broken the power of human censure and inner loneliness and fear, He turned her towards a more fulfilling life – 'Neither do I condemn you; go, and do not sin again.'

With others, our Lord made them face themselves in order to heal the effects of the past. The woman at the well at Sychar (John 4) must have had a degrading and painful life passing through the hands of six men. Her words have overtones of longing for something better (vv. 19–25). By confronting her with the nature of her life, Jesus was able to lead her to new hope.

Peter, particularly, is an example of our Lord's compassionate desire to heal a past which could have permanently blighted the remainder of his life. His denial of Christ at the arrest was a harrowing experience which must have shamed and broken him. Jesus ensured that this agony would be forever healed. He made Peter re-live that experience by repeating the question three times, 'Do you love me?' (John 21;15ff.). Peter re-affirmed his love for his Master, and knew that his love was accepted. Jesus confirmed that acceptance and His confidence in Peter by entrusting him with the commission 'Feed my sheep.' So the whole of Peter's sin, weakness and emotional instability was used by our Lord to open the way for Peter to give himself fully to His service.

If we add to the above outline of Christ's healing ministry the commonly emphasised connection of sin with sickness as in the cases of the paralysed man in Mark 2 and the man at the pool of Bethesda (John 5:14), and of sickness caused by Satanic activity (Luke 13:16), it is clear that our Lord's concern covered all forms of human sickness and suffering, whatever the source.

Christ's commission to His Church

Healing, then, was and is an integral part of Christ's redeeming work for mankind. This redemption only He can do, hence it is our Lord who heals. He continues His healing work through His Church, because the Church is His Body and He is its Head as Paul describes in Eph.1:22–3. Being such, the Church is 'the fulness of him who fills all in all.' The life and power of Christ is therefore the life and power of His Body. This means that our Lord's healing power is, since Pentecost, given through His Body.

In 1 Cor. 12 Paul speaks of the relationship which should exist within the parts of the Body if Christ is to use it effectively. Having said clearly to the Corinthians, 'Now you are the body of Christ and individually members of it' (v.27), he then goes on to point out (v.28) that 'the fullness of him who fills all in all' is expressed through His Body by the gifts of the Spirit who activates it. He is the One through whom the gifts are to be manifested – 'All these [the gifts] are inspired by the one and the same spirit, who apportions to each one individually as he wills' (v.11).

Paul sets out certain essentials of attitude in those who compose the Body if it is to function properly. These are, first, the recognition and acceptance of the fact that the Christian is not merely an individual but that he belongs to something larger than himself, i.e. Christ's Body (vv.15–20). It follows from this that, as in the case of the human body, each member of Christ's Body has need of the other members. Furthermore, each member himself has his own part to play for the good of the rest of the Body. Paul emphasises that this applies to all members, including those who seem to be weak or to have little to offer, or who appear unattractive (vv.21–4).

In order that all may be enabled to play their part, Paul says that the Body should be without discord, members sensitively caring for the needs of others. There is then created by the Spirit a fellowship where 'If one member suffers, all suffer together; if one member is honoured, all rejoice together' (vv. 25–6). In an atmosphere such as this Christ is able to work through His Body and the Spirit can manifest the richness of God 'for the common good'.

The Holy Spirit in our day is bringing back to the Church the understanding of its corporate nature as Paul describes it. For the carrying out of the healing ministry this unity in love is essential, as I hope will become clear.

No Christian may call himself a 'healer'. It is Christ who heals and He has commissioned His Church to act under His authority. 'And he called to him his twelve disciples and gave them authority over unclean spirits, to cast them out, and to heal every disease and every infirmity' (Matt. 10:1)

After His ascension, the infant Church realised and accepted this charge and prayed (after the release of Peter and John), 'And now, Lord, look upon their threats, and grant to thy servants to speak thy word with boldness, while thou stretchest out thy hand to heal, and signs and wonders are performed through the name of thy holy servant Jesus' (Acts 4:29–30). It could well be that any lack of 'signs and wonders' may, in part, be due to a failure to preach Christ as Saviour and Lord with its strong biblical emphasis on repentance. Such preaching should not be confined to the pulpit but be in the witness of all Christians, just as in apostolic times most evangelism must have been by individual witness.

Whatever may be the textual problems surrounding the end of Mark's Gospel, the fact remains that the words express what God expects of His Church: 'These signs shall accompany those who believe ... they will lay hands on the sick and they will recover ... And they went forth and preached everywhere, while the Lord worked with them and confirmed the message by the signs that attended it' (Mark 16:17, 18, 20).

Why are all not healed?

Any book on healing must face this baffling question. We do not always see 'signs and wonders'. Why? I do not know. There is no easy answer to the problem of suffering, a mystery centred in the cross.

One evening I was called out to a lady in the parish. Her house had wooden, uncarpeted stairs. She had slipped near the top and fallen down the stairs on her back, hitting each hard stair as she descended. When I arrived she was in severe pain and could hardly move. I laid hands upon her. As we prayed she had a vivid sense of the presence of Christ and was immediately healed. Later, when the local hospital arranged an X-ray, it was found that a bone in the lower part of the spine had been broken but the fracture was healed.

About a year later, the same parishioner had an infection. Again I laid hands on her, but this time, although both she and I were confident that there would be an immediate healing, she received only a blessing in spirit. The infection took its full course of about two weeks. Why was there healing in the first instance and not in the second?

A member of a conference at Whatcombe House (the home of the community to which I belong), asked for laying on of hands as she was due to enter hospital for a hysterectomy. In addition, from childhood she had had trouble from a hernia and her doctor had warned her that it might become strangulated. At the hospital she had pointed out that she had the hernia and it was agreed that, if possible, the surgeon would deal with it at the same time as the hysterectomy. In due course she went into hospital. When seen by the house surgeon before the operation she mentioned the hernia. He examined her and said, 'You don't have a hernia. You've never had one.' Through the laying on of hands she had been healed of the hernia for which we did not ask, but not of the hysterectomy for which we did ask!

Cases like these are puzzling, and we must face the fact that such experiences occur in the healing ministry. We cannot explain these things but they need not inhibit us. Our resolve should be to place ourselves as fully as possible in our Lord's hands. The right attitude is expressed in a letter received from someone in hospital who wrote, 'I also feel that whether I'm healed, have a minor op. or a hyster-ectomy – well, it's really completely beyond my control and completely in His hands, but He's going to bring the most loving answer out of the whole situation. What is tremen-dous is that I can write this now without a mental striving to have faith but a deep assurance that the Lord does love me and so can't act except in love towards me.' If a person in need of healing and those ministering could have this quiet confidence in the love of Christ, then we need not be too disturbed if we receive the unexpected answer.

There are many factors which inhibit healing. The sick person may not be ready for ministry either emotionally or as regards faith in God. If so, the Holy Spirit has not led us to pray for healing. Others still believe that God sends suffering either to purify or to punish. I am amazed at the number of times people say such things as, 'It's my cross, vicar,' or 'I'm a wicked man, and so I deserve this.'

A major reason for the lack of healing is that large numbers of Christians still do not believe that Christ will heal. At one period I was asked to take morning services during an interregnum. The first Sunday I noticed that the server suffered from asthma. The next Sunday I asked whether he had ever thought of having prayer for it. A look almost of fear came into his face and he immediately changed the conversation. This man, as is sometimes the case, could not even contemplate asking the Lord for healing. Others have reservations of different kinds, while large number of Christians believe that Christ *can* heal, but have not sufficient faith to believe that He *will* heal. Such weight of unbelief is bound to affect our ability to receive the healing love of Jesus. For this reason it is important that clergy and ministers instruct their congregation.

Sometimes there is unrealised or unrepented sin, or an unwillingness to forgive. A woman came to a healing service with chronic arthritis. As prayer was being made, God said to me by a word of knowledge, 'She must lose her bitterness.' I mentioned this to her but she refused to accept it. She left the church in a huff. Some years later, someone of whom she was very fond died. As she spoke to me about this it was clear that she was bitter against God for the death of her friend. To help release her from this attitude I reminded her of the word that had been given at the healing service. Her reply was, 'If God does this to me, I want nothing to do with Him.' She still has arthritis. God cannot act where sin blocks the way. The cause of physical suffering may be in the spirit or in the mind and healing will not be received until the underlying cause has been acknowledged and dealt with.

When praying for healing in the emotional life, in some cases one has to reach deep unexposed hurt. It may be that the person concerned cannot yet bear to look at what has been such a shattering experience, and so healing will be delayed.

We must also remember that the cause of trouble may be demonic rather than physical or emotional (see appendix on the deliverance ministry).

These things are mentioned to indicate that the ministry of healing is not necessarily straightforward. Many factors are involved and therefore, should there not be an immediate healing, we need not be discouraged. Jesus told us to persevere by asking, seeking and knocking and He gave us the parables of the man knocking up his neighbour at midnight (Luke 11:5–10), and of the widow pestering the judge (Luke 18:1–5). We are fighting the forces that spoil God's good creation and they may not give ground easily. There is no reason why we should not lay hands or anoint as many times as may seem necessary. As we do, we should ask the Holy Spirit to reveal the blockages.

If God wills all that is good we can trust Him whatever happens. Where healing is administered 'in an honest and good heart' God always acts to bless. Difficulties should not make us lose heart, but on the contrary force us into a closer life with Christ. Someone much involved in the ministry of healing once said to me, 'If I never saw one person healed, I would still continue this ministry because our Lord said we should do so.'

2

The ministering of healing

Prayer, confession and forgiveness, laying on of hands, anointing with oil and the Holy Communion are all means used by the Holy Spirit to bring the power of Christ to bear on our lives.

Prayer

When our Lord came down from the mount of Transfiguration He was met by a man whose son was possessed by an evil spirit. This man had brought his son to Jesus's disciples but they had not been able to heal him. After He had cast out the evil spirit, His disciples asked Jesus why they had not been able to do so. Jesus replied, 'This kind cannot be driven out by anything but by prayer' (Mark 9:29). Prayer is the basis of the healing ministry.

For Jesus Himself this was the case. His relationship with His Father was the means whereby mighty works could be performed. 'Do you not believe that I am in the Father and the Father in me? The words that I say to you I do not speak on my own authority, but the Father who dwells in me does his works' (John 14:10).

If His power is to come through us, prayer is as essential for us as for Christ. Prayer is the expression of a living

24

relationship with our Lord. Someone has said, 'Prayer is the way anyone gets into God's hands' and that is exactly what we have to do if He is to exercise His power through us. Our relationship with our Lord is parallel to His with the Father. Jesus expressed this in the words, 'I am the good shepherd; I know my own and my own know me, as the Father knows me and I know the Father' (John 10:14). When we have such an awareness of Christ within, then the way is open for Him to operate through us. This personal relationship with our Lord is the ground of our faith. The more we know, love and trust Him, the more we shall believe that He will do as He promised (John 14:12–14).

Prayer is at the heart of healing and this applies whether we minister singly, as members of prayer groups or in healing services. The power of God is released through prayer. Whether we minister or receive healing it is from the hand of God through prayer, be it through forgiveness, laying on of hands, anointing or the Holy Communion.

Confession and forgiveness

If we could trace illness to its source we would eventually find it in sin and evil. It may not necessarily be the sick person's own sin, for sins of society, heredity, environment and ignorance (to name a few) all affect health of body, mind and spirit. With all this, the individual shares the common sin of humanity from which he springs. We are 'born in sin'. Nevertheless, our personal sin, with the guilt which results, can be an important factor in our disorders.

The receiving of God's forgiveness is part of our healing. In helping others to wholeness, we are obliged to see whether sin remains to be dealt with. A great part of healing is often the joy and relief of receiving the forgiving love of Jesus.

In the present moving of the Spirit in the Church, He is leading us to a greater willingness to share. Many are finding the need to open their hearts to God in the accepting, loving presence of another or others. In this way griefs, hurts and sins which have for years been hidden because of fear are brought into the open and their power broken.

In personal ministry people are opening up their intimate lives in a way which is not always so when making a formal confession. The Holy Spirit is showing to people who would not normally consider going to a priest for formal confession and absolution the need to face and confess their guilt. In many prayer groups sharing is becoming an accepted part of their activity. This is not an emotional and immature attempt to taste the sordid. It is a desire to be right with God and real with people, to make mature relationships and to encourage and build up the members of the group in a frank, forgiving and accepting atmosphere. So the forgiving love of Christ is received to open up the way for healing.

Laying on of hands

Our Lord was not afraid of physical contact. He normally healed by touch. Either He touched people (Mark 1:31, 1:41) or people touched Him (Mark 6:56). We have only a few recorded instances in the Gospels of Jesus healing at a distance. In the case of the healing of the woman who had had a haemorrhage for twelve years (Mark 5:25ff.), it is recorded that 'Jesus, perceiving in himself *that power had gone forth from him*, immediately turned about in the crowd, and said, "Who touched my garments?"' When we are led by the Spirit to lay hands on a sick person for healing, we should expect the same flow of power from Christ through us. We specifically become the bridge between Christ and that person so that His healing can be transmitted. What a privilege this is!

To lay hands is also a salutary and adventurous experience. When we do so we pin-point our faith and dependence on Christ because we have before us someone who is trusting in the reality of both. Nothing, I find, drives me more into the hands of God in prayer than the challenge of this healing ministry. We should accept this challenge and opportunity for it is by stepping out in faithful dependence upon our Lord that we mature and learn how He wishes to use us. Just as the way to learn to pray is by praying, so the way we can be used to alleviate suffering is by stepping out with Christ.

With the laying on of hands the sick person is obviously involved. If one prays from a distance (for example, as a member of a prayer group) even though the sick person may be aware that prayer is being offered, the amount of involvement may be small. When, however, hands are actually laid on people, their expectancy and faith is clearly called out. This helps them to exercise both. They also have the aid and encouragement of those praying with them. Concentration and openness to the activity of the Spirit are essential if, in the laying on of hands, we are to receive the grace Christ gives.

Anointing with oil

Those who are from a sacramental tradition have tended towards the use of anointing with oil in the ministry of healing. This sacramental act is being revived among

Christians of all traditions. The use of oil as a means of grace is very ancient. In Old Testament times kings, prophets and priests had oil poured over them at their consecration to God's service. So anointing has usually been reserved for people who are known to be practising members of the Church. Another reason for limiting its use in this way is that, being regarded as a sacrament or a sacramental act, it has been part of the liturgical life of the Church. It is common for anointing to be administered within the context of the service of Holy Communion.

There is, therefore, with anointing a strong sense of the corporate nature of its use. In the Anglican Church and in other Communions it is the priest who performs the anointing and he does so as representing the Body of Christ. Some prefer to anoint with oil as, being sacramental, the personal element is less conspicuous. With the laying on of hands there could be emphasis put upon the person ministering. Be that as it may, anointing and laying on of hands are often combined.

In the New Testament anointing with oil for healing is mentioned only twice. It seems that our Lord instructed His disciples to do this when He sent the twelve out in pairs, for Mark records, 'And they cast out many demons, and anointed with oil many that were sick and healed them' (6:13).

The other instance is in the Epistle of James (5:13ff.). Here the sick person is instructed to call the elders of the church who are to anoint him with oil in the name of Christ. Two things stand out in this chapter. The first is that those who have the oversight of the Christian community together share the caring ministry to its members. This is being increasingly appreciated today and as this understanding spreads it could significantly change the atmosphere and image of the local church. The local church is the natural centre for the healing ministry. The Guild of Health is surely right in insisting that ministers and congregations should co-ordinate to make it an integral part of their church life. It may be necessary for individuals and groups in a congregation to pioneer the way, but they should be only pioneers. Ultimately, the whole congregation should be involved.

The second salient fact in James 5 concerns the confession of sins. In services for the anointing of the sick, provision is usually made for the confession of sins before the anointing. The apostolic pattern of James 5 is thus continued. However, in the passage it is said, 'Therefore confess your sins *to one another* and pray for one another that you may be healed' (v.16). This, too, is becoming a feature of church life, as described earlier. The Spirit is bringing us back to New Testament practice.

The method of anointing used in the Church of England is to dip the thumb in the oil and make the sign of the cross on the forehead of the person asking for healing. Some bishops arrange for oil to be consecrated at a particular time such as Maundy Thursday. The priest himself, however, may consecrate oil and the following prayer could be used:

O Almighty God who has taught us by thy holy apostle St. James to anoint the sick with oil in thy name, and that the prayer of faith shall save him that is sick; bless this oil we beseech thee, that whosoever may be anointed therewith may be delivered from all troubles of body and mind, and from every assault of the powers of evil; through Jesus Christ our Lord. Amen.

A formal service for the anointing of the sick is given as a note at the end of this chapter.

Holy Communion

Since Holy Communion is a sacrament, it is in itself the mediation of Christ's redemptive love. For those who believe that we receive Christ Himself – however that may be expressed – in the sacrament, then clearly the power to heal is included in the 'benefits of his passion'. The form of the words of administration in the Book of Common Prayer of the Church of England expresses the comprehensiveness of the sacrament where the receiving of the elements are said to 'preserve thy body and soul unto everlasting life'.

The Holy Communion expresses the belonging to the Body and hence the love and prayers of the Body. The receiving of God's grace together emphasises that the individual Christian is caught up not only in the love of Christ but also in the love and caring of the congregation who corporately minister God's grace. I believe that as we appreciate more the corporate nature of the sacrament, it will be increasingly seen to be a means of our Lord's healing work.

I heard recently of a parish priest at a Sunday morning Eucharist who asked for the prayers of the congregation for one member. The sick man was led to the altar rail by two members of the church in company with other communicants. As the priest gave the sacrament to the sick man and laid hands on him, the whole congregation enveloped him in prayer. He was instantly healed.

Here is another instance, this time in the healing of relationships between a married couple. The following letter is written by a Roman Catholic. Having described a period of very difficult relationship with her husband which came to a head while on holiday, she said:

Next day, we had a misunderstanding. I'd rather not describe it, but it seemed that we had reached the depths of how bad things could be. I didn't know how to be hurt more – I can only guess how he felt. This was the dreadful state of affairs just before we went to Mass one Sunday evening. We knew we couldn't go to Mass in that state but we also knew we couldn't *not* go. We needed the Lord more than ever. Somehow, again, by the grace of God, we were able to turn to each other just before Mass began, and wordlessly grasp one another's hand. When the time came, we went to receive Holy Communion. On receiving Holy Communion *Jesus healed all our hurt*. Not one scrap was left, not one painful memory. He gave us a new start and when we got back from holiday, no one would have ever guessed what a traumatic holiday it had been!

Relationship with the medical profession

In considering ways in which healing is administered in the Church, it is appropriate to mention the medical profession. There need be no conflict. If I cut my finger, the blood will in time coagulate and gradually the flesh will knit together and the cut will be healed. This is because the body has natural healing resources given to it by God. A doctor acts to facilitate the natural healing powers of the body. The same can be said of the surgeon and the psychiatrist. The latter's purpose is to help the patient realise his condition and its cause, and gain his co-operation to release inherent resources and so enable him again to embrace life.

In all this it is the God-given healing powers of the body and personality which operate. The medical profession are following God's laws even if members of it repudiate Him, and some of their methods and attitudes are questioned. Where there is co-operation with the medical profession, the result is great benefit to those who suffer.

In my last parish it was my good fortune to have two Christian doctors with whom I could work closely. We used to meet at the vicarage after service on Sunday evenings. This gave us the opportunity to discuss people in need. Their medical knowledge often proved invaluable to me and they accepted and used my ministry. We found this mutually encouraging and enlightening and we had the satisfaction of knowing that our combined knowledge and personal gifts, dedicated as they were to Christ, ensured that those whom we served were receiving from us the best we had to give. One of the doctors was also a psychiatrist, so we were able together to offer our Lord's healing on all three levels of spirit, mind and body.

This happy arrangement does not, I am aware, exist everywhere. There can be on both sides distrust, ignorance and sometimes downright criticism, but such attitudes may be broken down and co-operation encouraged. Since the medical profession is fast moving away from its former concentration on the physical aspect of healing and is realising the part that spirit and mind play in the life and health of people, there is hope that from their side co-operation with the Christian ministry will increase. Conversely, clergy and ministers must demonstrate to doctors that they have a power for healing from Christ which they can offer.

A service for the anointing of the sick

1. PREPARATION
Prayer.
A psalm e.g. 23, 121, 130.
A Bible reading.
   Suitable passages are:
   one of our Lord's miracles of healing.
   His commission to heal (Luke 9:1–2 and 6).
   James 5:14–15.

2. CONFESSION AND ABSOLUTION

CONFESSION
'I confess to God Almighty, the Father, the Son, and the
Holy Spirit, in the sight of the whole company of heaven,
that I have sinned exceedingly in thought, word, and deed,
through my own grievous fault. Wherefore, I pray Almighty
God, the Father, the Son, and the Holy Sprit to have
mercy on me.'

ABSOLUTION
'May the Almighty and merciful God grant you pardon,
absolution, and remission of all your sins, space for true
repentance, amendment of life, and the grace and comfort
of the Holy Spirit. Amen.'

3. ANOINTING
'I anoint you with holy oil in the name of the Father,
and of the Son, and of the Holy Spirit. Amen.
As with this oil your body outwardly is anointed, so may
our heavenly Father grant of his goodness that your soul
may inwardly be anointed with the Holy Spirit, who is the
Spirit of all strength, comfort, joy, and gladness. May the

Almighty Lord send to you release of all pains, troubles, and diseases, both in body and mind. May he pardon you all your sins and offences, and grant you strength to serve him truly; through Jesus Christ our Lord. Amen.'

4. CONCLUDING PRAYER
5. THE BLESSING.

3

Ready to be used

We can all be used in the ministry of healing. The twelve apostles were ordinary people, but it is recorded, 'Now many signs and wonders were done among the people by the hands of the apostles' (Acts 5:12). Similarly, the Apostle Paul said of the faithful ones who followed their lead, not many wise, powerful or of noble birth were called by God (1 Cor.1:26), but it is evident from 1 Cor. 12 that Paul expected the Spirit to work in power through them.

The Holy Spirit is showing that not only will He lead us into an intimate relationship with other members of Christ's Body, but also that the Spirit Himself can, and should, be powerfully active through us. In 1 Peter it says, 'But you are a chosen race, a royal priesthood, a holy nation, God's own people, *that you may declare the wonderful deeds* of him who called you out of darkness into his marvellous light' (2:9). We are, in fact, being given a richer insight into what the 'priesthood of the laity' means. It does not mean only that the spiritual work of the Church is not confined to the ordained ministry, but also that the laity should be used by our Lord for the kind of things listed by Paul in 1 Cor.12:8–10.

One does not necessarily have to be a Christian of long standing. I heard of the following incident. A Christian woman was involved in an accident in which she received severe injuries to her ankle. Her husband, also in the accident, was converted during the process of recovery. He asked for his wife to be prayed for at a local healing service but it was for some reason cancelled. So he prayed himself for her healing. That night she woke up feeling a burning sensation in her ankle, and was completely healed. This is not to suggest that maturity counts for nothing, but basically what our Lord requires of those who share the healing ministry is a willingness to live in an intimate personal relationship with Him in loving obedience. Three things are necessary: prayer, a holy life and faith.

Prayer

We now consider prayer as the way by which we are prepared by God to participate in the healing ministry.

Julian of Norwich told us in *A Shewing of God's love* how prayer makes the soul one with God. She added, 'For it is God's will that we pray, and to this He stirs us in these words aforesaid. For He willeth that we be full sure that our prayer shall be answered; because prayer pleases God. Prayer puts a man at peace with himself, and makes him serene and meek who was before in strife and travail.' So God stirs us to pray, answers the prayer we then make and gives us that serene and meek spirit through which He can speak and act. Julian's words beautifully express what should be our experience in prayer, and they encourage us to aim at the loving oneness with God which breathes in her writings.

Julian says of God in another place 'our Lord is so homely and courteous'. In saying this she is teaching us that we should be our natural selves when we pray. I once heard words something like this:

It is easier for you to be close to Me,
If you promise to be yourself.

This naturalness is delightfully expressed by Brother Lawrence in *The Practice of the Presence of God*. He says, 'That when he had failed in his duty, he only confessed his fault, saying to God, "I shall never do otherwise, if You leave me to myself; 'tis You must hinder my falling, and mend what is amiss." That after this, he gave himself no further uneasiness about it.'

In our prayer we do not need to copy anyone else or try to fit ourselves into a pattern. It may help to use a set form or some system such as A C T S – adoration, confession, thanksgiving, supplication – in that order. If so, that is how we should pray. But if we can better express ourselves by using our own words, or as a result of meditating on the Bible, then that is how we should pray.

We need to pray naturally in the sense of bringing our whole self to God. How tiresome if we try only to present to God those parts which we think acceptable to Him. We should bring both good and bad, for He knows about the parts of which we are most ashamed or disappointed. So we come and present our whole selves for our Lord to make new.

We should also be honest with God about how we feel. If we are feeling that we do not want to pray, we should tell God that – and still pray. It is the same if we are resentful or angry. We come to God offering ourselves in the condition that we are. Then He is able to act within us and deal with the needs our attitude reveals. Nothing should hinder our coming to God. Our Lord showed us the truth of this in Gethsemane. He came to His Father with the honesty that He did not want to face the cross, 'Abba, Father ... remove this cup from me.'

When Jesus taught about prayer He said, 'Do not heap up empty phrases as the Gentiles do; for they think they will be heard for their many words. Do not be like them, for your Father knows what you need before you ask him' (Matt. 6:7–8). We do not need to say a lot when we pray. There is no necessity to convince or coax God. A great amount of activity on our part is not required. What we are required to do is so to put ourselves into God's hands, that He is able to act according to His perfect wisdom and love. We have to remember that what matters most in prayer is what *God* does. This, after all, is why we pray. It applies whether He is to receive our adoration and thanks, to work within us or to answer our requests.

It is important in prayer to be relaxed, with inner peace and sensitivity to God. I believe that most of us are able to use a contemplative form of prayer if we practise fixing our minds on the Lord. We can do this by, first, being in a comfortable position, able to forget our bodies. As they become relaxed, we can then quieten our minds, letting work, worries and problems slip away. Then, fixing our attention on the Lord Jesus, we repeat silently or quietly His name in order to keep our attention on Him. Some will be able to pray in tongues. As we do this, we become accustomed to 'being' with our Lord, asking nothing of Him, but resting in His presence and learning to be receptive to Him. Wandering thoughts must not disturb us. We need constantly to bring our attention gently back to our Lord whenever it has moved away from Him.

Prayer requires, as Jesus taught, a determination to persist. 'When you pray, go into your room and shut the door and pray to your Father who is in secret' (Matt. 6:6). We have to cultivate the discipline of getting away on our own to be with God. The discipline of meeting with God regularly in prayer was emphasised by our Lord in the two parables of the persistent neighbour and the widow and the judge.

Have you heard of praying in the Spirit (i.e. in tongues)? When we pray in tongues we do not use our own words. The words that we speak are those given to us by the Holy Spirit. He speaks a language unknown to us through our lips. This means that we are able to concentrate wholly on God Himself, not on the words we think or say, because the Spirit is praying His prayer through us. When we pray in tongues for someone who is ill, we take that person to Christ in the Spirit's prayer, leaving our Lord to act as He wills. This is in line with Paul's teaching in Romans 8:26, 'Likewise the Spirit helps us in our weakness; for we do not know how to pray as we ought, but the Spirit Himself intercedes for us with sighs too deep for words.' As the Spirit Himself prays through us when we place a person in Christ in this way, we can be sure 'the Spirit intercedes'. His prayer is too 'deep for words'. That is, it is deeper than our understanding can fathom. At times we may have the experience of His 'sighs and groans' as we share His deep prayer.

Holiness

Sin, obviously, will be a barrier between us and Christ and so, if we are to be used by Him, we will want Him to free us from the sin barriers that exist. If two people love each other, they long to be as close as possible. Barriers cause grief. Such should be the relationship between our Lord and ourselves.

Holiness is thought by some to be a hard righteousness. This could not have been so with Jesus. Sinners flocked to Him. The prostitute in Luke 7 came to him *because* He was holy. There was nothing off-putting about our Lord's holiness. It was attractive. It must have been seen as true purity of motive with no strings attached; a transparent goodness and genuine caring unsullied by the selfishness, greed and ambition of normal human life.

The Holy Spirit is described by Paul as 'the Spirit of holiness' (Rom. 1:4). We should therefore ask Him for the desire to become a holy person. The holiness He will give us is the attractive holiness of our Lord. It is an important moment in our growth in the Spirit when we are given the desire to be holy; to be clean, pure vessels of God with clear and unmixed motives, and with an overriding desire to be a fit temple of the Holy Spirit.

This means that we shall take sin and repentance seriously. It does not follow that we become introspective. Rather we ask the grace of the Holy Spirit to see ourselves as He sees us. If we really want this, He will show us as much as we can bear. We can trust Him not only to convict us of our state of sin, but also to move within us at the moment we behave in thought or act in a way that grieves Him. So we make Psalm 51 our prayer. 'Create in me a clean heart, O Lord'. This He will do for us. He will not allow us to wallow in our sin, but as He convicts, so will He give us the assurance that He is doing what we have asked.

He may well lead us to weep over our sin at times. Not until I was baptised in the Holy Spirit did this happen to me. It must have been more common among Christians in earlier times, for the Roman liturgy had a 'Mass for the gift of tears'. The collect is as follows: 'Almighty and most gentle God, You caused a fountain of living water to gush out of the rock in order to quench the thirst of Your people; draw from our hardened hearts tears of compunction, that we may be able to mourn for our sins and seek their forgiveness from Your mercy; through Jesus Christ our Lord. Amen.'

Such weeping cannot be fabricated; it is not an outburst of emotionalism. The Spirit moves within us to bring us to a penitence which can be expressed only in tears. It is a refreshing, freeing, cleansing experience. Many people need to weep. The putting up of barriers and presenting a bold face to the world only increases the internal agony of past guilt and suffering. When we open our heart and let the pain be expressed, so often this comes out with a flood of tears and sobs. In a counselling room one essential is a box of tissues.

The whole point of holiness is to be 'oned with God' as Julian said. Our Lord taught, 'Blessed are the pure in heart, for they shall see God' (Matt. 5:8). It is this longing to 'see' God which drives us to holiness. It is therefore very positive. Far from being a fixation on sin, it is the reaching out of the soul to God so that one lives in the joy of His forgiving love. An incident which demonstrates the true nature of repentance is the one previously referred to, of the prostitute who came to Jesus when He was invited by Simon to dine at his house. This woman wept and was forgiven because 'she loved much', that is, she loved Jesus so much. Her actions and tears expressed both her sorrow for what He exposed in her and her love for what she saw in Him and the two drove her to His feet. Jesus accepted both unconditionally.

So, desire for holiness is the action of love for God within us which drives us into Christ's arms. This resulting union makes possible the flow of His healing love to those in need. Care regarding thoughts, eyes and tongue is clearly necessary. We should try to nip in the bud anything which dishonours God by asking Christ immediately to enter into such things and cleanse them. The Spirit longs to give us a love for our Lord which would make us hate to grieve Him or break the union we have with Him. So we aim, by God's grace, to make the atmosphere of our life one of constant walking with Him.

Faith

It seems from the New Testament that our Lord asked one thing only of those who begged for healing. That was faith that He could do it. He was able to evoke faith and so people flocked to Him because they believed He could heal them. The leper cried out, 'If you will, you can make me clean.' His words express the attitude of all the others who came to Jesus for healing.

With some He said explicitly that their faith was the means of healing – 'Daughter, your faith has made you well' (Mark 5:34). On occasion He first established that faith was present before He took action to heal. He asked the two blind men, 'Do you believe that I am able to do this?' When they answered, 'Yes, Lord', He touched their eyes and said, 'According to your faith be it done to you' (Matt. 9:27ff.). When the four friends brought the paralysed man to Jesus, Mark records, 'And when Jesus saw *their* faith, he said to the paralytic, My son, your sins are forgiven' (Mark 2:5). It is encouraging to know from this that a sick person is able to rely upon the faith of others for his healing. So we can have confidence that our faith will be used by Christ for the healing of others. At other times our Lord required demonstration of faith: 'Stretch out your hand', 'Rise, take up your pallet and walk', 'Go, your son will live'.

Since our Lord demanded faith in this way, it follows that faith is required of us also. Prayer and holiness are obviously paramount here, for they join us to Christ. The more real He is to us, the more we have the conviction that He hears and acts. Many, perhaps most, of us find that it is the definite act of praying with people for healing which develops our faith. This seems to be what the author of Hebrews is saying to us in chapter eleven. The great figures of the past of whom he speaks and presents as illustrations, demonstrated their faith by acting in obedience to God's command to them (Heb. 11:8). So with ourselves, it is our obedience to Christ's charge to heal which demonstrates our faith. At first we tend to pray, 'If it be Thy will' in a rather indefinite way, but as we continue in this work, we learn to speak more positively. We are able to say to our Lord something like this, 'You have commanded us to do this, and we praise You that at this moment You are giving Your healing grace to Your servant as You have promised.'

What we trust in is not merely our own amount of faith, but in Christ and what He has said. We do not pray for the sick because we think we ought to, but because Christ has told us to do so. We act upon that. Any doubts or hindrances of faith which we may have we plant firmly in His promises, fixing our attention on what He commanded and pray in the context of that.

We need not be disturbed if our faith includes some element of doubt. If we had absolute certainty, there would be no faith involved. Like the father of the boy with the dumb spirit in Mark 9, we say to our Lord, 'I believe, help my unbelief'. That is to say, 'I *do* have faith in You, Lord, and I leave You to care for any unbelief that may exist in me.' Anthony Bloom in *Living Prayer* puts it this way, 'When we say, "Yes, I doubt, but I do believe in God's love more than I trust my own doubts", then it is possible for God to act.'

So we step out expectantly, looking to Jesus to do some lovely thing. The words of 1 John 5:14–16 are helpful, 'And this is the confidence which we have in him, that if we ask anything according to his will he hears us. And if we know that he hears us in whatever we ask, we know that we have obtained the requests made to him.' In saying this, we do not overlook that there is a *gift* of faith. This will be mentioned in chapter five.

As we grow in faith that Christ will act, so we are able to evoke faith in others. It is not for us to demand too much of a sick person because his very illness can weaken his response to God. We should remember, also, that it is often easier to have faith for someone else than for oneself. So we need to have an infectious confidence in Christ and in this way to stimulate the sick person's faith. In any case, praying with others usually gives an impetus to faith.

Some people rely increasingly upon the leading of the Spirit before they minister healing to a sick person. Agnes Sanford has described how she moved from praying indiscriminately for anyone who asked, to praying for healing only when prompted by the Spirit. Others also will not act unless they have the inner conviction of the Spirit or else feel in their arms and hands a sensation which they recognise as the touch of the Spirit.

One evening at Whatcombe House we had a meeting for prayer and teaching for members of the local church. As the people were leaving, one lady said to me, 'I have to go into hospital soon for an operation.' As she said that, I felt a tingling sensation in my hands and forearms and thought I ought to ask her, 'Would you like us to pray for you?' 'Oh, please,' she replied. My wife and I laid hands on her as she sat in a chair with her head bowed. Suddenly, as we prayed, her head shot up and I knew she had been healed. She knew it, too. She said, 'I have heard of this happening to other people but I never thought it would happen to me.' That was over three years ago and she has had no return of the trouble. This incident illustrates that, as mentioned earlier, the faith of those ministering can evoke that of the sick person.

After having prayed with someone, we can leave it to God to act in His own way. He may heal immediately or over a period. The healing may begin to take effect within a day or two. He may do unexpected things. God alone knows all the circumstances of the case and the needs of the sick person. There may be good reason why immediate healing is not given. I remember one occasion when I was ill. Hands were laid on me by members of the community, and we could not understand why healing was delayed. However, as I lay in bed, God began to speak to me about a question of relationships. By His leading it became possible to face this squarely, to repent, and to clear the matter with the person in question. Within hours the symptoms disappeared and I returned to normal duty. Many cases could be cited where immediate healing was not given, but for very good reason. Nevertheless, the fact remains that in some cases there appears to be neither the healing we seek nor the reason for its absence.

It can even happen that during or after the laying on of hands the pain may at first intensify. One instance of this occurred when my wife was suffering with sinusitis. As we were praying, the pain became so acute as to be almost unbearable. This continued after prayer for a time, but gradually the pain subsided and within an hour there was a complete healing and inner peace.

There are problems in the healing ministry, but where prayer is made in the love of Christ, He always blesses. We learn a lot, not by dictating to God (albeit unconsciously), but by seeing how He acts in each case. Should there be need for further ministry, we may administer this, co-operating with what our Lord is doing. If only, say, one in ten is healed, that is a significant percentage, but there is no doubt that a much higher proportion are appreciably blessed.

Fasting

Many Christians involved in the healing ministry are feeling the urge to fast. They are learning to use this form of discipline in order to be more effective in God's hands and they are finding it beneficial both as regards their spiritual life generally as well as at times of special concentration of prayer.

Fasting is a particular form of abstinence. In some parts of the Church abstinence from certain pleasures and indulgences is practised in Lent. Such things as smoking, alcoholic drinks, sweets, sugar, coffee and tea are commonly given up during that period of six weeks. Fasting is total abstinence from all food (but not liquid refreshment, except in unusual circumstances).

Why do we fast? Overall it is that we should be a better channel for God's purposes. We have the desire to serve Him fully and fasting appeals to us in that it can be an effective way of attacking our weaknesses. We use it against our fleshly nature – to pommel our body and subdue it by bringing it more under control (1 Cor. 9:27). It is also a means of developing a more disciplined life, for it militates against our natural tendency to become self-indulgent. In addition, it is a help to our prayer. It can give it an added incisiveness as well as making us more alert. It is common knowledge that food has a dulling effect upon the mind. When we abstain we are able to be more fresh mentally.

We may fast as a general discipline, or for particular reasons as they arise. With the former we decide on a regular pattern of fasting, such as every Friday up to the evening meal. This then becomes woven into our spiritual life in company with prayer, Bible reading and worship. Others prefer to fast for a definite object. When a request for prayer comes, the decision will be taken to fast in addition. So, for example, it may be felt right to fast for two days. The time normally spent in eating will then usually be given to extra prayer.

Fasting is, our Lord indicated, a matter between God and the individual. 'When you fast, anoint your head and wash your face, that your fasting may not be seen by men but by your Father who is in secret' (Matt. 6:17). In view of this, our decision to fast should be taken according to God's direction, whether it be as a general discipline or for a specific purpose. This is important since to fast is for most people demanding. When we are convinced that we do it at the direction of God, we have sufficient incentive to carry it through.

It is sensible when we first embark upon fasting to give ourselves the opportunity to become accustomed to it. To attempt too much at the outset can mean the disappointment of failure. We may initially forego one meal and use the time for extra prayer. After some experience we should then be in a position to miss two meals or to abstain for the whole of a day. There can be some discomfort. A slight headache is not unusual, the breath may smell and we may feel a certain weakness. For most people, these effects do not hinder normal activity.

It may be well to give a warning against feelings. The efficacy of fasting should not be judged by emotional reaction. I remember embarking on a three-day fast, anticipating that I would have a rich spiritual experience.

Quite the reverse was the case and at the end I felt a strong disappointment. A few days afterwards, however, I was aware – in a way I cannot describe – that God has used that fast to give an inner blessing.

Fasting is not a discipline most people accept, but we would do well to ask the Holy Spirit to make us sensitive to His leading on the practice. A fuller treatment of the subject is given in *God's Chosen Fast*, by Arthur Wallis (Victory Press).

4

Prayer for physical healing

The majority of those taking part in the Church's healing ministry do so as members of a prayer group. One of the effects of the in-filling of the Spirit is the immediate increased desire to pray. Not only does the Spirit give a richer consciousness of God within, but with this comes a longing to pray with others. The 'fellowship of the Holy Spirit' becomes a need and the fellowship a fellowship of prayer. To be effective members of a prayer group we do not have to be 'super' Christians, but we must mean business and learn to trust in the Holy Spirit. This we can all do, and that is why we have given some attention to personal prayer, holiness and faith. A prayer group can be a powerful instrument for God, so it is well to give some consideration to its functioning. It can also be a source of encouragement and growth to its members and is often the means by which they first are used in some form of ministry.

What is to follow will assume the existence of one or more prayer groups in a church, charismatic or otherwise. Should there not be such a group and it is desired that there should be one, a book such as *The Charismatic Prayer Group* by John Gunstone (Hodder and Stoughton) will be found useful not only in the matter of starting a group but also in the running of it.

What a group can be

A group is a cell of Christ's living Body. It should regard itself as moving under the hand of the Head of the Body. Each member should know and love Christ and long to be used in His service. And so, above all, God should be worshipped for Himself by the group. That intent should be at the heart of all activity. There will then be a strong sense of God's presence and faith that He answers prayer. If this is the case, there will be an atmosphere of praise and joy. One of the refreshing actions of the Spirit today is that He is bringing back into our prayer and worship this welling up of thanks, praise and joy.

With the vertical attitude towards God right, the horizontal relationship can be right also. The group has the joy of learning to become a unity in the Spirit. The Holy Spirit works to bring a group into this oneness. Such a unity does not come at once. It is a gradual growing together in trust and openness. None of us finds it easy to drop the barriers we have built up over the years in order to protect ourselves from hurts, but to be able to do so is a great release and brings a warmth and fellowship for which we all long. When we do have the courage to admit to others what we really are and what the effect of life upon us has been, we usually learn with surprise that we differ little from others. To share also gives the members of the group the opportunity to enter into the suffering and needs of each other and give the benefit of their own experience. The group is able to learn to minister to each other.

As such they can become committed to each other as well as to Christ. Nothing draws people together more than an atmosphere where one is able to be truly oneself. I heard of a group, the leader of which was an ex-missionary of long experience who, on returning to this country, became a lay reader in her church, playing a leading part in its life and being greatly respected. One evening at her prayer group she poured out the anguish of her heart. She admitted that she felt spiritually dead and quite unable to pray, resentful towards God and to some people. There was a momentary silence as the other members recovered from the shock and then they all responded from their hearts, surrounding her with love and a desire to bear with her in her distress. A member of the group said, 'From that moment we became a group instead of a set of enclosed individuals.' It is a rich experience to be a member of an accepting group.

Growing together can have its bad moments. As we reveal our true selves we are bound to expose things which displease and hurt others. Our own views, attitudes, habits and beliefs will sometimes cut across those of other members of the group. To be prepared for such situations requires a determination to learn a new depth of accepting and loving. It also calls for a willingness on our own part to realise what effect we may be having on others – something of which we may be blissfully unaware, and with this, a willingness to hear a thing or two for our own benefit with the accompanying desire to be changed. Such things have the beneficial effect of showing us our need of God and so of forcing us to lean on Him.

One of the less commendable aspects of church life is that so many are unable to be their real selves. We have been brought up to put on our 'church face', which means, in effect, that there must be no disturbing of our relationships. Disturbances due to jealousy, pride, worldliness and position-seeking we do have and these are an affront to God and a shame before men, but disturbances caused by allowing others and ourselves to be real should be the outworking of the Spirit of truth. The Holy Spirit can be a most disturbing Person. As He moves within and among us He can make us grow in patience, kindness, gentleness and self-control in our dealings with each other.

What a tragedy in a congregation when few are aware of the griefs, disappointments and heart-breaks hidden just below the surface of many lives. This is because members of a congregation do not 'meet'. Groups can give us the opportunity of finding and appreciating the real person. As such, we may approach the picture drawn for us by Paul, 'If one member suffers, all suffer together; if one member is honoured, all rejoice together' (1 Cor. 12:26). God give us the grace to lose our dread of others seeing us as we truly are!

My wife received a telephone call from someone in the parish. This person said, 'Lucia, since you have been living here you have become someone I love deeply, so much so that it has become the most precious relationship I have. But you do not know the real me and I love you so much that I cannot bear to carry on a friendship which, from my side, is false. I must see you and tell you the truth about myself.' My wife asked her to come over and when she did she poured out her heart with many tears. When she had finished, my wife said, 'This is wonderful. Now I can love the real you.' A relationship like that is unlikely to break because it is founded on truth and love.

In our small groups we can learn, perhaps cautiously, to lose our fears of being real and at the same time learn to love in a fresh way. Our groups could be places where we are trained by God to notice the suffering around us and meet it.

The right intention of the members

Although a prayer group can develop the potential of its members and meet their personal needs, our motive for joining should be that we may serve our Lord and be a channel of His healing. To play our full part as a member, we must be prepared to be involved in the prayer. This will entail a disciplining of our spiritual life, including honest self-examination both of ourselves and of our relationship with God and with others. It may also involve visiting those for whom we pray, to be open to the Spirit's prompting for the manifestation of His gifts, and may be to lay hands on someone.

It is the willingness to be involved which brings to us the awareness that the Spirit is using us and gives the stimulus we need to venture further. He never demands more than we can give.

Most groups have periods when they seem to be in decline. Then there has to be a willingness, if need be, for the group to submit to some self-examination. If a group wishes to serve with the right motive it will face these times positively and honestly. Possible causes are that a slackness has come upon its members; that relationships may be wrong, or it may be that the personnel of the group has changed too much or too little. A group can be too large. Twelve should be a maximum. Above that number it should split.

Other difficulties can be poor leadership, one or more members dominating the prayer and discussion, or conversely, an unwillingness by some to contribute. Whatever the cause, the Holy Spirit should be asked to reveal it. When the obstacles to growth are recognised and dealt with, the group will mature and become increasingly useful in Christ's hands. No Christian group exists without its ups and downs, so it should not be despondent when difficulties come. We are all learners, and have need to rely on God.

To make the group effective for God and a rich experience for its members there should be advance preparation. Each member should at home pray away any wrong relationship, attitude, upset or hurt which could spoil the quality of the prayer. So the group should be able to enter without hindrance into unimpeded concentration on God. The more a group grows in the Spirit, the more sensitive is the atmosphere to wrong attitudes. A member who is bitter or jealous can affect the atmosphere strongly. If this is so, the leader should call the group to order and ask the offending member to put himself right with God. This need not entail mentioning names.

At times a cloud descends upon a group which is not caused by the condition of the members. This may be the action of evil powers. If so, the leader needs to use the authority given to us by our Lord and command the evil influence to depart. If done in faith, the oppression clears at once.

It may be well to mention that the deep unconscious parts of us are as involved in our prayer as the conscious. We may be quite unaware of powerful prayers which are our deep, unspoken longings. These may conflict with our conscious prayer. It is essential, as mentioned earlier, that Christ be taken into every part of our being to unify us and hence our prayer, conscious and unconscious.

The group's prayer

The prayer of a group can easily become superficial. It may

consist of running through a list of several names, giving a short time to each. There is a need to go more deeply if we are to make it possible for the Spirit to act, and ourselves to be in attentive co-operation with Him.

Be sensitive to God. Ample time should be given to allow the Spirit to lead the group into a rich quietness. Be unhurried so that the Spirit may be free to speak through prophecy, vision, or from the scriptures. This often leads to praise, thanksgiving and adoration. The group may equally be brought to contrition and repentance or be challenged by God. Such times have a formative effect, since the consciousness of the presence of God so produced makes the prayer alive and the members in a state of expectancy.

Having allowed the Spirit to create such an atmosphere, the group may then bring Christ to those in need of healing. Again, there should be no hurry. One person should be brought in prayer to the touch of our Lord with enough information to the members as will allow them to enter into the suffering and so evoke compassion in their hearts. The needy person should be held into Christ by the group with as strong a concentration of prayer and love as possible.

Some may be helped by picturing the person enveloped by our Lord, or by thinking of Him laying hands. For certain people such picturing is of no help, but they concentrate on linking the sick person with Christ. However group members pray their aim is to hold the one for whom they are praying in the love and power of Christ who is present among them. As he is taken into the hands of Jesus, members of the group should be alert to the Spirit so that He may speak or act.

The deeper someone is held in the healing love of Christ, the more He is able to do for that person. As the members of the group grow closer, the ability to continue in prayer is made easier, because the group develops a common heart.

The length of time each sick person is held in prayer must depend upon the leading of the Spirit. Often the group as a whole is aware when to cease praying, but otherwise the leader must decide.

If it is praying for someone present, the group has the joy of surrounding that person with the love of Christ and hands can be laid on him in the confidence of the combined strength of the love and faith of the members. The group can learn to rely upon the Spirit as to whom is given the privilege of laying hands. Members should respond without self-consciousness to the prompting of the Spirit. Sometimes He uses one person, at others more than one.

Group prayer like this, with personal ministry to one or more present is something we need to develop in our church services. The Spirit can generate in a congregation a sensitivity and compassion for the sick and sorrowing among them. Such people can be lovingly supported and so be able to open their suffering to the healing love of Christ. When I was a curate I was told that it was said of me, 'He's not a real vicar, only an apprentice.' Our groups should be places where we work out our apprenticeship. They are ideal for this. Within them we can minister to each other without being paralysed with fear in case we make a mistake. This is one of the ways in which groups can support and enrich the life of the congregation.

Whatever information is released to the group should be treated as confidential. If there is a breach of confidence the group will get the name of dealing in scandal.

Individual ministry

Since the bulk of the spiritual ministry of our churches has been left to the ordained ministry the laity has become reserved, feeling themselves inadequate and often, with good reason, untrained. This reticence has to be overcome, and so most of us need to be eased gently into the healing ministry. If this applies to clergy and ministers, as it does in many instances, it must apply even more to those in the pew.

Ministering needs in no way to be 'official', governed by ritual, or a special heavenly certificate. One day a parishioner came to me quite excited. She said, 'Two days ago I went to see Mrs. A. You know she's been in bed a couple of weeks. As I was sitting there I felt I should hold her hands. After a short time I asked her, "Shall we have a prayer for your illness?" I felt a bit awkward asking, but to my surprise she said, "Oh! thank you, dear. I was hoping you might suggest that." We prayed and there was such a sense of peace. I saw her again today and she is so much better. She's up and able to do things for herself.' Another person told me that she accompanied a friend in an ambulance to hospital to have, as she thought, a shoulder bone reset. As they travelled to the hospital, the friend put her arm around the patient and prayed. After being examined, she was told that the bone did not need re-setting.

These two instances show how naturally and unobtrusively the laying on of hands can be given. It is not essential to place one's hands on a person's head. Incidentally, touch in itself can be a comfort as well as a means of grace. When visiting sick people either at home or in hospital they are often helped just by having their hands held. To put an arm round someone who is ill can be a warm and welcome action. To pray when we do so seems to follow naturally. Anyone can be used by our Lord for such caring ministry. To give us confidence, we may at first pray for minor troubles such as a common cold, a wasp sting or a headache. It helps to pray for one's own small illnesses and see our Lord work. This builds our faith.

Here are some comments of a practical nature when praying for the sick:

1. Find out whether the sick person is able to co-operate. Do not force prayer on people.

2. Do not hurry. Take time to be composed. Fix one's attention on Christ and open oneself to the flow of His love.

3. Be sensitive to the Holy Spirit who may wish to guide or speak.

4. Pray as positively and naturally as you can, realising we have the authority of Christ. *He* heals.

5. Do not decide what God will do. See what He does and co-operate in the process of healing if there is not an immediate recovery. Lay hands and pray as many times as necessary.

6. Tears sometimes come. If so, allow them to be expressed till peace returns. Sometimes they are tears of relief or gratitude.

7. Thank God at the end of the prayer that He has heard and answered.

8. After prayer, do your best to explain that the healing of the body is part of the whole loving action of Christ. That to receive Him into the heart as Saviour is the full healing. For those already committed to Christ, this may be the opportunity to re-affirm and deepen life with Him.

9. If a priest or minister is attending the sick person, the laying on of hands or anointing may be performed within the service of Holy Communion. A lay person may accompany him or a group may be praying in church as he ministers.

We need to allow the sick person to be at ease so that he may take his part fully in the prayer. He may be apprehensive or may not be able to prepare himself adequately. In such a case pray quietly over him, asking for the tranquillity of Jesus and help him to place himself trustingly into the hands of our Lord.

When all is ready and prayer is to be made, those ministering should place themselves by or around the sick person. When only one is ministering, he or she should take as comfortable a position as possible. If the sick person is in bed, it may be best to sit in a chair. When more than one is present they may place themselves round the patient, either with hands outstretched towards him or touching him lightly. Should the sick person be in a chair or prayer is made in church, it may be best to stand behind him, laying hands on head or shoulders. Others assisting may do likewise. Hands should be laid lightly, particularly if placed on the head.

All should then concentrate on Christ, opening themselves as channels of His healing. The prayer offered should be that which is natural to those making it. It is well to remain in a state of prayer after the actual request for healing has been made, in order to be open to God's leading. A recent experience will illustrate the need for this.

Two of us were asked to pray for a lady who had a severe back condition. She was attending hospital daily for traction. The previous day she had received some relief by this treatment, but on the day she came to us there had been no alleviation. She had been ill for some time and much prayer had been made already, so as we began to minister, our faith was not strong.

However, as we prayed, both of us sensed the presence of God and, feeling a gentle leading of the Spirit, did our best to respond. After some time, the lady ministering with me said she had a picture in her mind of an old lady carrying a burden on her shoulders. She was bent nearly double, yet all she needed to do was to put her burden down. My companion said, as she told us of the vision, that she felt it referred to the sick person's family problems, and that the burden of them should be given to God. We asked her to try to do this and she co-operated as best she could.

Shortly afterwards I felt a strong urge to move my hand down her spine, pressing strongly as I did so. We prayed as this was being done, for the love and peace of Jesus to move upon her. Suddenly her back muscles, which had been so taut, began to relax. The Spirit then indicated the centre of tension and with my hand there, we prayed for the healing love of Jesus to radiate out to the whole of her back. More release of the muscles followed and they became soft. Then we felt strongly that we should urge her to rock from her hips backwards and forwards. At first she did this with some hesitancy but as she felt no pain she increased the motion until she was moving freely.

I am sometimes asked, should we pray for someone who is unconscious? One evening I was called to a patient in hospital. The sister informed me that the doctors did not expect him to last the night. At his bedside the nurse in attendance said that he had lost consciousness, having consecutive fits. Within half an hour of laying hands on him the fits ceased and next morning he was able to sit up in bed. I was told of a minister visiting a hospital who laid hands on a patient in a coma and prayed for him in tongues. A few days later, when the patient had recovered consciousness, he told the minister that he knew he had been prayed for.

It is clear from these instances that though the conscious mind is inactive, the unconscious or the spirit is alert. 'Spirit to spirit speaks.' Through prayer Christ penetrated into the unconscious and so was able to heal. Someone who is unconscious may not offer resistance to prayer as could be the case if conscious. In the first instance mentioned above, the patient would have understood little of the ministry of healing, have had minimal faith in God and would have been embarrassed had he been aware that hands were laid upon him. He was able to receive God's healing when unconscious in a way that would not have been possible if conscious.

This is not to say that there can be no resistance by the unconscious mind. With many people, the strongest opposition to God emanates from it. Much would depend upon the condition of the patient as to whether healing would come to an unconscious person, but the above two instances may overcome any hesitancy we may have of praying for someone who has lost consciousness.

It is not uncommon for clergymen or hospital chaplains to pray with an elderly unconscious patient and be told shortly afterwards that he died peacefully in his sleep. Did the prayer penetrate the unconscious mind and enable him to release himself into God for the final 'healing' that awaited him?

5

The Spirit and physical healing

In a remarkable way God is giving to His Church a new awareness of the Holy Spirit through what is called the Charismatic Renewal. With this has come a more conscious reliance on the Spirit and a new understanding and experience both of the fruit of His in-dwelling and His gifts. One of the gifts is the healing gift (1 Cor. 12:9). The experience called the 'baptism' or 'fulness' or 'release' of the Spirit which is becoming widespread, should mean an increase of compassion for suffering humanity and also an expectation that we can be used by God to alleviate it.

Once we have been given the in-filling of the Spirit, we should be prepared to be used for any of the gifts, including that of healing. It is not a matter of whether we feel worthy or not. It is the Spirit's prerogative, as Paul teaches us, to decide whom He will use and when: 'All these are inspired by one and the same Spirit, who apportions to each one individually as he wills' (1 Cor. 12:11).

It has been said that the Spirit can be as disturbing as He is renewing. The baptism in the Holy Spirit does not mean the end of problems. Some books give an over-simplified impression – be filled with the Spirit and all will be well. After the in-filling with its joy, the Spirit gets to grips with each of us. He will move into areas which we have attempted to shut off from God or of which we have been hitherto unaware. This will at times be painful, and so He has to baptise us into sorrow as well as into joy. One person who experienced this to a strong degree wrote, 'I believe that I have come out of the long tunnel which I seemed to enter when Jesus baptised me in the Holy Spirit.' When He fills us we become aware that He takes control of the whole of our life as bit by bit He works to cleanse and renew.

Here we touch on His work only as it affects the healing ministry. When the Spirit moves within us, He deals not only with our physical nature but with sin, hidden hurts, fears, relationships and emotional states which may underlie physical symptoms. When we co-operate with Him, we can be healed and released. If we resist, it can lead to suffering and bewilderment; it has been known to end in breakdown. In such cases the Spirit clearly indicates that we must give attention to root causes before healing can come.

Generally speaking, we should realise that the in-filling of the Spirit is not a heavenly magic wand. It in no way obviates the discipline of the Christian life, nor causes us to escape the suffering and difficulties of the hard road (Matt. 7:14), nor of the normal lot of humanity. But He does give us a new joy and expectancy, with the assurance that God is at work within us in a richer way than ever before.

This I know from my own experience. As an incumbent I did my best to serve both God and people. But hard work, much prayer, hours of visiting, care with taking of services and preaching did not give the spiritual power to my life that I needed and longed for either personally or in my ministry. It was when I learned that Christ has the function to baptise us with the Holy Spirit (Mark 1:8) that there came a change. I had prayed earnestly the Confirmation prayer, that I might daily increase in the Holy Spirit more and more, but though, no doubt, the Spirit was not inactive, the evidence of His presence within me did not accord with what I read in the Acts of the Apostles and the Epistles.

When Jesus filled me with the Spirit there came a new consciousness of the Spirit's presence and I knew Him in a personal way. In my life a change gradually took place. From being negative and apologetic I became more positive. Love and joy for which I had so longed began to be felt. After a time I knew the breaking of some besetting sins. Two desires were felt strongly, one for deeper fellowship with other Christians and the other, to witness for Christ. My personal ministry became more effective with some of the gifts of the Spirit operating when there was need. All this, naturally, affected the life of the parishes and, as an increasing number of lay people entered into this experience, so God worked more deeply in their lives, enriched our worship, and began to open up a new phase of growth in our Lord.

For all of us the enriching by the Holy Spirit can make our life in Christ more purposive, productive and full of hope. For the ordained it can mean a transformation in their ministry, God at work through them in a way they had not known before.

The Spirit's guidance

It has already been mentioned that guidance to minister may come as an inner impulse or a sensation in the hands and arms. It may also be felt as an 'anointing'. That means we are aware of a strong presence of the Spirit upon us and with it the recognition that He is about to act.

When we pray with the sick, we keep attentive to the Spirit. Should a vision be given, we describe it. If a prophecy or word of knowledge or wisdom, we speak it out.

We then act upon what is said. So the Spirit will guide the form and content of our prayer. It may happen that there is no strong lead from the Spirit. In that case we pray as it seems right in the circumstances. As we have already committed ourselves into the Spirit's hands, we can be confident that it is still He who is making our prayer.

On occasions we are led to lay hands on other parts of the body than the head or shoulders. We should be sure of our guidance here for obvious reasons. Nevertheless, I have seen a remarkable work of Christ when truly so guided. We prayed for a man with a badly injured knee which had not responded to treatment and was giving much pain. Strong pressure came from the Spirit to place my hands on the front and back of the knee. Almost immediately the knee returned to normal.

Again, may it be said, learning to be led by the Spirit is a slow process. We should be willing to go the road of all learners, knowing that we may make mistakes. It helps, for example, to say as we speak a prophecy, 'I think God is saying ...' Or, if a word of wisdom or knowledge comes, 'I believe the Spirit is indicating ...' We then leave it open for others to test what comes. As Paul says, 'Let the others weigh what is said' (1 Cor. 14:29).

We should never give the impression that we have a 'hot line' to heaven, and most certainly not secretly so believe in our ability to hear the Lord that we border on infallibility and resent any questioning of what comes from us. If what we say is truly from God, it will witness as such to the hearers.

The gifts of the Spirit

We should now say something of the gifts of which we have

been speaking. It is true that more than one list of gifts is given in the New Testament and even these do not cover all the richness of the Holy Spirit's gifts to us. We concentrate on those in 1 Cor. 12 because the Spirit is bringing these into prominence today and our experience shows that they are used by Him in the healing work of the Church, be it physical or emotional.

THE WORD OF WISDOM

This, like the word (or utterance) of knowledge, is 'given'. That is to say, it is not something we do, expressing our own wisdom or knowledge, but some wisdom or knowledge given to us by the Spirit. It may be a word from scripture which is appropriate to the situation. To someone whose marriage was in jeopardy, God gave the word, 'What therefore God has joined together, let not man put asunder.' It was the last advice she wanted, but the marriage was saved because she accepted this from God.

The word of wisdom may express some truth of our faith (cf. 1 Cor. 2:6–13). A man trying to find his way to God was speaking of his problems. He could accept the greatness of God but not His interest in an individual person. I blurted out, 'But God is your Father!' When I said it, it felt as though I had made a trite and unhelpful remark. Later the man said that it had made God personal to him and opened the way for him to become a Christian. 'The foolishness of God is wiser than men' (1 Cor. 1:25).

THE WORD OF KNOWLEDGE

At times, as we minister to someone, information about them is given to us. The Spirit speaks, telling us something relevant to the person's condition. As hands were being laid on a lady for healing of arthritis, the Spirit said, 'She has a deep bitterness.' When challenged, the lady at first denied this, but later admitted a bad relationship with her sister. She bitterly resented her sister's behaviour and this had smouldered for years. The facing, repenting and healing of that bitterness led to the alleviation of the arthritic condition.

On another occasion, as hands were being laid on a lady, the Spirit said in a word of knowledge that she was suffering from a congenital spinal malformation and that she needed to put right a certain relationship. Later she was found in tears. These tears were tears of joy, for the word of knowledge given through a member of the community was precisely the opinion stated by the consultant she had seen a few weeks previously. Now, however, for the first time for years, she could stand straight up without pain.

FAITH

The *gift* of faith differs from the normal life of faith in God because it is a definite act of the Spirit in a particular situation. When it operates, it means that God gives an absolute confidence that a healing will take place. Acts 3:4-7 seems an instance of this. I remember vividly an incident one Easter Day. An urgent telephone call came during the afternoon asking me to visit a home in one of my parishes. As soon as I was free I went to the house to find the father sobbing and his wife laughing hysterically. He was a pig farmer. Foot and mouth disease was active in many areas and the farmer had placed a large trough of strong carbolic at the farm gate. After lunch his two-and-a-half-year-old daughter had been present as he fed the pigs. After a time he became aware that she was no longer with him. He rushed to the front of the house. When he reached it he saw two little red shoes sticking out of the trough, with the rest of the little girl in the disinfectant. He snatched her out and raced her to hospital.

When I arrived at the house and had quietened the couple somewhat, I prayed with them. As I did so I knew in my spirit that all would be well and that their little daughter would suffer no ill effects. So I could pray, 'Lord, I know that this child will return home untouched.' When, four days later she came back home, her eyes, ears, mouth, skin and lungs were in perfect condition.

GIFTS OF HEALING

Through prayer, the Spirit uses a person or persons to heal the spirit, mind or body of someone in need. Most are used for this gift at irregular intervals but some have a continuing ministry and may be led to devote their lives to this service. St. Paul uses the phrase 'gifts' of healing, in the plural. This may mean that He will use certain people for specific kinds of illness. One man said to me that he was used almost exclusively for arthritic and rheumatic complaints. Another may be used primarily for the healing of emotional disorders, another for spiritual needs. It may also be that this would apply to the medical profession – specialists in various diseases and psychiatry.

PROPHECY

While we are ministering, God may speak a word of prophecy. In this, we are aware that words are being given by the Spirit and as they come, we speak them out until the words cease. Often a message is one of comfort or for the revealing of the condition of the person being prayed for. One day we prayed for a lady whose neck was so affected by arthritis that it was virtually locked. As we prayed, the Spirit said, 'I will reveal to you the cause of this trouble.' At three a.m. she awoke and knew the circumstances which caused the arthritis. Over a short period she was fully healed.

DISCERNMENT OF SPIRITS

More will be said of this when we consider healing of past sufferings. In that case the Spirit discerns for us the condition of the human spirit. Here we may mention His action regarding evil spirits. With this gift, He can make us aware of the presence and action of evil powers, or that they are somehow involved in the suffering. The action of evil spirits is a large subject and books describing this ministry exist, so little will be said here. An appendix on the deliverance ministry is given at the end of the book. Unless we are sure that God is leading us into such ministry and we have strong evidence of His power in it, we would be wise to refrain from involvement.

PRAYER IN TONGUES

Praying in tongues or in the Spirit as it is sometimes called helps us to be conscious of God's presence and to be ready to respond to His leading. It is helpful to pray in tongues at the commencement of and during ministry. We should, if possible, prepare for ministry beforehand and when doing so, prayer in the Spirit can form some of the preparation as the Spirit leads us to concentrate on our Lord and so be in His hands.

Many are hesitant when asked to consider themselves as channels whom the Spirit may use for His gifts. One often hears diffidence expressed in such ways as, 'I'm not good enough' or by the question, 'Is it really the Holy Spirit or is it my own idea?' Some are held back by fear, 'Suppose nothing happens?' Such reactions can be inhibiting, even paralysing. If the Holy Spirit is to work, we must be willing to take the plunge. Of course we are not good enough; of course we could mistake our own feelings for the Spirit's touch, and if we have made a mistake, nothing may happen.

It seems, however, that the Holy Spirit is not so perturbed at the possibility of error. What He requires is an adventurous spirit which will do its best to be sensitive to what God may be indicating, and then step out faithfully. How otherwise are we to learn to respond to the Spirit? So I urge Christians truly to believe that, as Paul teaches us, the Spirit 'apportions to each one individually *as He wills*'. Any of us may be the one He chooses to use. It is better to make a mistake, trusting the Spirit to teach us, than to let inhibitions block the activity of God. A desire to meet the needs of those who suffer is one of the best antidotes to inhibition.

Useful books are available which give full descriptions of the gifts of the Spirit. Just the bare essentials as relating to the healing work of the Church have been given. In the operation of the gifts we are completely dependent upon the Spirit. We should never attempt to force them, but should have the desire for them so that we may be ready whenever the Spirit moves.

6

Involving the congregation

As we emphasised in chapter one our Lord gave His healing ministry to the Church as a whole. Congregations ought to be involved and presented with the obligation and privilege of taking part. This may be difficult since for too long a time congregations have expected to leave ministry in spiritual matters to those who are ordained.

Teaching the congregation

Effort and persistence will be required on the part of clergy and ministers if the Christian in the pew is to be encouraged to take his part. The aim should be to help lay people to regard this healing work as a part of their lives as members of Christ's Body. They need to grasp the vision that what Christ did on earth He still will do through His Church.

It is the privilege of the minister to teach his people so that they may know how to take their part. He will need to cover a wide range. The following summary may be of use in his planning of the teaching:

1. Teach that all healing is of God.
2. Explain the effect of being spirit, mind and body, i.e. that sin and emotional disorders affect the bodily

condition and vice versa. Healing must therefore be for the whole person, and is part of salvation.

3. Point out the wrong ideas people have about illness:
    (a) That God sends it as punishment for sin.
    (b) That it is 'my cross'.
    (c) That death is a disaster.
    (d) Deal with the fear of the supernatural. Many Christians see the faith only as a moral code and have a fear of supernatural action by God.

4. Teach that the Church is Christ's Body e.g. 1 Cor. 12, Eph. 4. Link the congregation with our Lord's work by describing:
    (a) The facts of Jesus's healing ministry.
    (b) His commission to the Church.
    (c) The work of the Spirit in the Body of Christ.

5. Expound the healing miracles of our Lord.

6. Teach about faith and encourage it.

7. Teach how to pray for healing in groups and individually.

8. Explain how they can themselves receive healing:
    (a) The need to believe in Christ's present, living action and that He wants to heal.
    (b) To open themselves as fully as possible to Him, confessing the sins that resist His work in them.
    (c) They must not only ask for healing, but actually receive it into themselves.
    (d) They should 'see' themselves well again from the moment of being prayed for.
    (e) If they do not receive immediate healing, they should daily take our Lord into their whole being as they pray, so that He may continue and complete His healing work in them.
    (f) It will help them to meditate on positive words e.g. 'I am the Lord, your healer' (Ex. 15:26); 'For I will

restore health to you and your wounds I will heal, says the Lord' (Jer. 30:17); 'Whatever you ask in my name, I will do it' (John 14:13); 'The power of the Lord was with him to heal' (Luke 5:17).

9. If possible, describe recent healings. Sometimes arrange for personal testimonies from those who have been healed.

Clearly this will involve a series of sermons. It will also be necessary to repeat the teaching at regular intervals, because to many people this will be an entirely new subject about which they will have reservations. Patience will be required, gentleness and a quiet persistence, as well as a lot of individual encouragement. One of the best ways of helping members of the congregation is to persuade them to join small groups. So much can be done in groups by actually taking part in prayer for healing. Healing services will help, and these we will now consider.

Healing services

Healing services have problems, but there is no doubt that under proper control and with instruction they have a part to play in the local church. It is difficult to deny that some people are given by the Spirit a special function to conduct healing services, since there is evident demonstration of the power of God working through them. Some people react emotionally against such services, but this should not prejudice us. It is also true that some such services may be so emotionally charged that it is questionable whether the Holy Spirit is truly in control. Given due care, however, healing services can enrich the life of the church and we should not be apprehensive in making them part of our life.

Before we do so the congregation should be well instructed. There should be a significant number who are able wholeheartedly to take part. The prayer groups of the church are clearly important here. Given this, the minister should be able to weave the healing ministry into the total life of his church.

This can be done by using the normal Sunday services. In doing so, the healing commission of the Church is stressed as well as the corporate nature of it. It demonstrates that the whole congregation is to be concerned in it, not just the few 'who feel that way'. People who would be diffident if asked individually to take part in some healing activity are able to do so as members of the congregation present when they see people actually being given this ministry.

The Holy Communion is for some the obvious service, not only because it represents the full action of Christ for our salvation (of which healing is a part), but also for the practical reasons that the ministry can be fitted naturally into the worship. In Anglican worship, various parts of the liturgy may be used. In the Book of Common Prayer rite, two places are appropriate:

1. When people receive the sacrament.
2. Immediately after all have received.

In Series 2 and 3, there are three suitable places:

1. At the intercessions.
2. When people receive the sacrament.
3. Immediately after all have received.

In non-liturgical services, ministry could follow the address. This would be appropriate since teaching would lead easily into action. The same may be said of Morning and Evening Prayer. The place of the intercessions could be used, the address being brought forward to serve as teaching preparation.

If the Communion service is chosen and there is a large number requiring healing, it can cause difficulty administering at the communion rail. In some churches there are enough clergy for one to be free to lay hands or anoint. In such a case (or when there are only a handful desiring ministry) it is possible for this to be given at the rail at the same time as the congregation comes to receive the sacrament. Then those requiring healing remain after having received the sacrament so that the minister assigned may lay hands or anoint.

When there is only one clergyman it is not usually practical to minister at the time of distribution of the elements. He may invite those in need of prayer to come to the rail at another point of the service. He may then more easily invite lay people to assist him. This is equally the case if individual glasses are used. Suitable lay readers, deacons, elders, P.C.C. members, or others of the congregation involved in the ministry of healing, could be invited to do so.

This not only trains them. It also means that the Holy Spirit has more people who are prepared to be used and so develops the potential of the church. The Spirit may indicate those who are to be used. Such people may be sent to pray with the sick of the area – too many for the local ministers to serve adequately. Using lay people also has the practical benefit of shortening the service.

Some who minister prefer the people to remain in their seats and to pray for them altogether, asking those in need to accept the healing of Christ as prayer is made. This is done to put the emphasis upon God's action rather than upon the minister. It encourages those asking for healing to receive direct from the Lord without reliance on any intermediary, but the fact remains that the laying on of hands is for many a boost to their faith.

When praying with the sick the minister may either use the same formal prayer for each one or he may prefer to act in a more individual way. If formal prayer is preferred, one for anointing is given in chapter 2. Here is a shorter prayer:

I anoint you in the Name of the Father, and of the Son, and of the Holy Spirit. Receive the healing of the Lord and His blessing. Amen.

For the laying on of hands, the following prayer from the Archbishops' Commission on Healing (1958) is suitable:

Our Lord Jesus Christ, who gave commandment to his Church to heal the sick, of his great mercy make thee whole: and by his authority committed unto me I lay hands on thee, that thou mayest be healed of thy infirmities, in the name of the Father, and of the Son and of the Holy Ghost. Amen.

If a more personal approach is desired, each one is asked to describe his need. An extempore prayer is then made. In whatever way prayer is offered, the Holy Spirit may give a word of knowledge or wisdom, or move by discernment or prophecy. In such ways the Spirit reveals causes of sickness or factors involved in it. A prophecy may give encouragement to the sick person or guide his future behaviour or attitude.

Prayer of an extempore kind more easily allows for others to assist. If two or three are praying for someone, though one will take the lead, the others will also be attentive to God and will contribute what He gives to them in word, vision or prophecy as well as by their support by faith. Obviously this way of ministering will take longer, but it is to many more satisfying. The need to use lay people is thereby underlined. If enough suitable people are available, two or three pairs may minister simultaneously.

There can be physical manifestations when hands are laid on people. With some who minister, their hands shake and they continue to pray until the shaking ceases. With others, some of those receiving ministry may fall as if unconscious. In many instances there is an awareness of warmth or sometimes of coldness, while others feel as though an electric shock has passed through their body. These manifestations should not be taken as a sign of special outpouring of grace by our Lord, though they may no doubt be an assurance to those who have them. Experience shows that healings just as effective are performed with little or no physical sensation being felt. On the other hand, it would be wrong to suggest that there should be any attempt to suppress them.

Prayer for the sick by proxy is practised at times. A person asks for the laying on of hands for someone else who is sick. I have seen this to be effective and there appears to be no reason why it should not be done. The principle is the same as that of individual or group prayer for the sick who are not present. As we hold in our heart someone in need of God's grace, he is joined by us to Christ who is within and so God's grace passes to that person. The laying on of hands or anointing can add power to the prayer. Biblical precedents are the centurion's request for his servant (Matt. 8:5ff.), and that of the Syrophoenician woman for her daughter (Mark 7:25ff.). In each case Christ healed at the request of someone who had come some distance from the sick one. Matthew makes the point that the centurion's servant was healed at the very moment our Lord pronounced him cured (v.13).

When weekday services are arranged, the congregation should be encouraged to attend, to provide strong prayer backing. The healing prayer groups will provide much of this. Their experience of prayer is of great value not only to create an atmosphere of love and expectancy, but also because they should be accustomed to concentration in prayer for a fairly long time. This helps others who are in the habit of praying corporately only for the few minutes of intercessions normally practised in Sunday worship. At healing services, should there be a reasonable number requiring ministry, the congregation may be required to be in a state of prayer for upwards of an hour. A hymn and a Bible reading may provide a break.

Here is a form of service which could be used apart from the normal acts of worship. Such services are normally of a simple nature with concentration on those who come for healing. The opening period of prayer is important as this sets the atmosphere of the whole service. The aim should be to create an awareness of God and raise the faith of those present. An aid towards the latter is to read a verse or two of scripture which is positive and faith-building, followed by a period of silence which allows the congregation to absorb the words. The note of praise and thanksgiving should be prominent, not only during the early prayer but throughout the service. Hymns and choruses may be included. Two publications which have a useful compilation of both hymns and choruses are *Sound of Living Waters* and *Fresh Sounds* published by Hodder and Stoughton in both music and words editions.

Form of service for the laying on of hands

1. PERIOD OF PRAYER
   Aim: awareness of God's presence and to raise faith.
   Bible passages to help faith:
   Matt. 7:7–11, Heb. 4:14–16 and parts of chapter 11.
   Luke 4:18–19, 1 John 5:14–15.
   Include praise and thanksgiving.

2. THE LESSON
   Suggestions: 1 Kings 17:17–23, 2 Kings 5:8–14,
   Isaiah 35:1–6a, parts of chapter 53.
   The healings of Jesus.
   Acts 3:1–16, 9:32–42, 14:3–10.
   Rom. 8:14–17, 12:9–21.
   Eph. 3:7–20.

3. OPEN PRAYER (if desired)

4. A PERSONAL TESTIMONY OF HEALING (if possible)
   Short and to the point.

5. THE ADDRESS

6. THE LAYING ON OF HANDS

7. CLOSING PRAYERS AND THANKSGIVINGS

Those who are called to minister should prepare beforehand. Jesus taught this clearly at the healing of the boy
with the deaf and dumb spirit. When the disciples asked
why they had not been able to deal with the boy, Jesus
answered, 'This kind cannot be driven out by anything but

prayer.' Jesus had Himself just returned from prayer in the silence of the mountain. He could say to the boy's father, 'If you can! All things are possible to him who believes' (Mark 9:23).

As our Lord's own power came through His prayer-union with His Father (cf. John 14:10), so ours must come from our prayer-union with Him. Those who minister, ordained or lay, should set aside a time for prayer and quiet with God before ministering. The amount of time spent and the form of preparation will depend upon the individual concerned. Those most used in this work insist upon the importance of the preparation.

Fasting may be included. If the ministry is to be given during a morning service, abstinence from food could be practised until after the service. If one is preparing for an evening service, it would be beneficial to fast from after lunch. These are merely suggestions.

As members of the congregation see Christ at work through services in which they participate, they accept this ministry as part of the commission our Lord has given us, and their faith grows as they see Him touch and transform lives. This gives impetus to the whole of their life in Christ, and their attitude becomes positive, expectant and with the note of praise.

What are the dangers? Some who come for prayer may understand little about either the Christian faith or the healing ministry. They may be unprepared emotionally or spiritually. That being the case, the address should make clear the essential elements of the Church's ministry and of the cross and what this means in total salvation.

There is not the same opportunity for individual attention at healing services, with the danger of superficial ministry and disappointment. It may be possible to have a word with those who have received ministry, if there are experienced people available to do so. Should the numbers coming for healing be small, it is not so difficult to recognise strangers and it may be possible to follow up the laying on of hands with personal attention.

The advantages outweigh the disadvantages of such services, provided care is taken and good teaching is given. Churches should be prepared to ask the guidance of God as to whether the time is opportune for such development. Consideration of emotional needs around us, which we will begin to discuss in chapter seven may have an important bearing on such a decision.

7

Emotional healing: listening

So far, though we have regarded the healing ministry as 'wholeness', we have concentrated more on the healing of physical symptoms. Nowadays it is increasingly clear that many illnesses and diseases have behind them as a contributory cause, sometimes the whole cause, an emotional disturbance. It is, therefore, necessary for us to look behind the physical condition to the underlying emotional or spiritual state.

By bringing Christ's healing, not only is the emotional suffering dealt with, but also the physical which results from it.

The effect of modern life

Much illness can be traced to the conditions of modern life. We live in an age of rapid social and political changes which raise more problems than they solve and which carry with them industrial and international unrest. These affect the lives of everyone. Newspapers, radio and television daily feed us with disturbances from every part of the globe. The problems of the world are on our doorstep. Fear of redundancy and the stress of the 'rat race' dog the lives of many, while constant moving of house is making it difficult for large numbers to put down roots, as well as placing a strain on marriage. This leads often to its breakdown. If we add the questioning of previously accepted religious beliefs which has taken away from a large portion of the population both the reason for living and a moral code, it is not surprising that a loss of security torments – consciously or unconsciously – millions and has brought in the age of the tranquilliser. The stress of life today is exposing weaknesses which in previous, more settled conditions, were contained.

Noise is a new major cause of concern, and since so many seem unable to exist without it, it is at the same time a sedative and an irritant. Time has become a taskmaster and the pressure of it is a major cause of the tiredness which is a constant burden to an increasing number. Tiredness makes us vulnerable to influences we would otherwise ride over; problems become too large and decisions difficult. Pressure of work has much to blame for tiredness. As a result of the excessive demands of business and profession, it is not uncommon to meet those who have become unable to cut themselves off from their work and relax. The saying 'All work and no play makes Jack a dull boy' is only too true, but with an ominous element. Men in their thirties are having heart attacks. A doctor said to me, 'They'll be having them in their cradle soon.'

These things, with others as detrimental, must be in our minds as we help people back to wholeness. It may sound platitudinous to say that the answer is to lead people to a faith in God or to bring them back to a faith they have lost. Since the world has no final security in itself, we need to lead people to the only true security, which is God. We may be able to alleviate a situation by relieving pressure, but in the end it is a person's ability to *face* life with its pressures, sufferings and uncertainties that is their true healing. Only a power distinct from themselves and the world can do this for them, and only the same power, the Holy Spirit, knows the way by which each one can be led to Himself. Those of us, then, who would be used for such service have to learn to be sensitive to the guidance of the Spirit.

The deeper needs are in the realm of the emotional life. These include the inability to accept a new and demanding situation, or are due to some shock or deep anxiety. However, it is in the field of relationships where the most damaging things happen. The greatest injury to our personalities and our deepest reactions are caused by the way people behave to us. We are undermined by lack of security, causes of which may go back to infancy. The relationship we have with our parents, within our families, and with people with whom we become particularly involved, have the strongest effect upon us. If these are deficient of love we experience rejection, we believe we are unwanted, and this can cause the future fear of loneliness to gnaw at our lives.

Relationships effect our deepest emotions. Love, understanding, generosity and sacrifice can flower within them. But we can also be tormented by anxiety, fear, guilt and inferiority, as well as fostering sins of jealousy, resentment, pride, hate and revenge. What we suffer through our relationships has also a direct influence on our relationship with God. It may drive us into His arms and through suffering we may allow Him to effect deep changes in us, teaching us things about Himself and ourselves which previously we had been unable to see. Conversely, one meets those who complain that God does not care and who ask, 'Why do I have to suffer like this?' The bitterness drives a wedge between them and God, undermining worship, prayer and feeding upon the Word of God.

More will be said of this later. For the present let us

accept that all around us are people suffering from stress and wrong relationships and that this has its effect upon the body. Most people will talk about their physical ailments when they are hesitant of speaking about their inner selves.

A soldier has described how, at the fall of France in 1940, his unit was retreating to the coast, when suddenly German aircraft appeared and began to machine gun the road. When the attack had ended he found himself on the wrong side of a twelve-foot wall. In his terror he jumped the wall. This is an exceptional instance of the dramatic effect strong emotion can have upon the body. We recognise this fact in the more usual experience of a dry mouth when we are called upon to speak in public, or by saying 'it took my breath away', 'my heart sank', or when something causes us to have a sudden loss of appetite.

Our emotional life can affect every part of the body – blood, digestion, glands, nervous system, skin, muscles, joints etc. The result can be an ulcerated stomach, a heart attack, blood pressure, strokes, colitis, backache, migraine, disturbances in the reproductive organs, rashes, arthritis. When someone complains of such troubles, we realise there is likely to be an emotional cause.

Deprivation of love can cause depression for long periods, or the dark cloud may descend and then lift again within a few days. Some are caused to cling to others for constant support. Others become critical and hard, or conversely, spineless and appealing. A sense of inferiority is almost certain to be there although this may be camouflaged by a bumptious attitude. Such conditions may become intensified, leading to a breakdown or a psychotic illness.

The need

While the average minister or layman may not be equipped to deal with the more serious states, there is a wide and increasing demand which they are able to meet. This is for those people who feel the strain of modern life and who may also have emotional problems, but who manage to keep going, even though the strain may be quite difficult. They are not likely to become chronically ill, but they need an ear, someone who will listen and share their problems and give support and encouragement.

There are a great number of Christians who feel inadequate. They think they have little to give in service to others, but in fact they can do much. They can learn to *listen*. It is not required of them that they should attempt to become amateur psychiatrists, or even to act as a counsellor, but simply to become a 'listening post'. The things said in this chapter regarding listening, and what is to follow, are intended to assist them to do this.

All around us are people whose great need is to talk to someone who will listen sympathetically. They live in a world which seems either too busy and preoccupied to pay them any attention or is indifferent to their needs. Consequently, they have to nurse within themselves problems, fears and hurts which, unshared, increase in size and create loneliness. If, however, they are able to share they can experience a sense of release, the difficulties become reduced and they can see life more positively. It may mean that the listener is required to do no more than listen. Having a sympathetic and patient ear may be all that is required. How often, after doing just this, someone has said, 'I feel so much better now.'

We may not realise the needs around us because so many

hide their sufferings behind a calm and competent exterior. The fact that they have to do this indicates the need. It is easy to misinterpret attitudes which cover hurts, shame or inadequacies. Living under such a strain, they cannot be their true selves. So they can be misunderstood. A lady who had been living in a certain locality for about a year was thought to be a widow. She had the reputation of considering herself superior to her neighbours, hard and unfriendly. It was later found, when she was able to open her heart to someone who came alongside her, that her husband had left her. She had moved from her previous home in an effort to hide her shame. Soon after moving, her son had been convicted of embezzling money from his firm. She lived in the agony that her secrets might become known.

This woman's need was not for a psychiatrist or other professional help. It was to unburden her sorrow and any neighbour with the true spirit of Christ could have helped her. The opportunity to unburden her heart came because a sensitive and loving person noticed that she was suffering from an arthritic knee which affected her walking. After the sharing of her burden the two were able to pray for the healing of her knee.

The variety of suffering is extensive. In our attempt to come alongside people we have to do our best to see their problems as they do, not as those problems appear to us. Whatever their situation, however, they will not dare to reveal it until they meet someone who they believe not only to be understanding, but also to be trusted with confidences.

The listener

To be trusted not to repeat a confidence is a necessary condition of being a listener. Our attitude should be that we are in the hands of Christ who has given us a concern for others. If our hearts are so set, not only will a breach of confidence be an abhorrence, it will cut across the nature of the call. Such a breach would be an act of self-indulgence, whereas our concern is solely for those we serve, to bring them to know the love of Christ and their fulfilment in Him.

Neither shall we be in the category of those who 'need to be needed', and who therefore force themselves on to others for the wrong, albeit unconscious, motive. Such people have not come to terms with themselves. If our motive is to be solely under Christ, then we shall be people who are genuinely desirous of facing ourselves, life as it comes and, above all, our Lord.

If we are like this, we shall create an impression upon others which will make them feel that they could turn to us. It will also mean that at our first meeting with them, though the conversation may be of a rather superficial kind, we shall attentively and caringly listen to what they are saying. Such an attitude will encourage them to speak of more intimate matters in due course. We can trust the Holy Spirit to lead those to us whom He so desires. As we are sensitive to Him, so we shall learn to recognise those He brings.

When they come, above all we must *listen*. That is to be our major part. We let them talk while we enter as understandingly and imaginatively as we are able into what they are saying and expressing. Our concentration is to try to understand what it is like to be *them*. We can do this only by listening. We need to be silent even when there are periods when they are not able to say anything. As we listen and accept them without judgement, even in our hearts, they will be able to pour out their grief.

It may be that after hearing all that a person has to say, something of our own experience may be brought to our mind by the Spirit to comfort, encourage or maybe to suggest uncritically. It can help to share our own experience. Be that as it may, our main concern is to allow the one who comes to release the painful things trapped within.

At times there may come expressions of emotion. The person may begin to sob, or be in an agony of suffering. He may blurt out his real feelings about someone who has injured him. We need not withdraw from strong expression of feeling but rather share it, staying with the person in his agitation and calmly covering him with the love of Christ. The working through of deep hurts may be a lengthy business, with a tendency by some to return often to a particular suffering.

This will mean that, having been given the care of someone by God, we are content to continue with that person as long as is necessary. Clearly the question of time is involved. To be used as a listener is bound to make demands, so we must be prepared. It may require a change in our priorities and activities, so we may find it necessary to pray these through. We must not take on more than we are able to contain.

If we belong to a prayer group the encouragement and prayer of its members can be a strong support. Other members of the group may also have more experience and it may be necessary on occasion to pass someone over to them or to our minister. We should not, of course, discuss the affairs of those with whom we are involved without having their approval, but our listening may disclose a situation which we are not competent to manage, and so we have to direct this to others more experienced.

In any local church the ministry of listening could develop into a kind of 'listening centre'. This does not mean an organisation which might well cause problems, giving the impression of a gossip centre. Rather it could be that members of a church feel a corporate awareness of need around them and become open to the flow of the love of Christ. This would mean the sharing of the burden so often planted solely upon the shoulders of the ordained ministry (and their wives!). In addition to those with hidden suffering there are the sick, the bed-ridden and terminal cases, the aged and the lonely. All these need an ear and the breath of the love of God. Not only is it obvious that the ordained ministry cannot cope with the situation today, but the Spirit is reminding us again that as the Body of Christ, we are all involved in the ministry of love He has given to His Church.

Those in Christ are able to help others because they have a security independent of this world. This does not mean that they feel self-confident, nor that they are freed from the agonies, frustrations and problems which are the human lot. It does mean that they have an inner life that is built on Christ who is not governed 'by the changes and chances of this fleeting world'. This is the Christian's tranquillity and we have the privilege of guiding others into the same life. We can help them hear Him say, 'Come unto me, all who labour and are heavy laden, and I will give you rest. Take my yoke upon you, and learn of me; for I am gentle and lowly in heart, and you will find rest for your souls' (Matt. 11:28–9).

As we serve in this ministry of listening we may find that much present suffering has its roots in the past. Painful memories require healing if there is to be that release which will enable someone to embrace and enter into life freely and hopefully. As the Holy Spirit uses us to minister to others by listening, He may also desire to use us for the release of the past. This is often called the 'healing of the memories' or the 'healing of forgotten pain'. For this we need to understand something of how the human personality functions.

8

Emotional healing: conflict

In thinking of wholeness, we need to remember that we are
'one whole'. This is the case not only because body, mind
and spirit are mysteriously and wonderfully related, but
because all that we have experienced from conception to
the present time is 'one whole' and combines to make us
what we are.

The conscious mind

A large part of what has happened to us throughout our
lives we are able to remember. We prefer to remember the
pleasant and enjoyable things and try to forget the painful
experiences, but good and bad are all part of our consciousness and we have the ability to bring them back to mind
when the need arises. We enjoy reminiscing over happy
times, but many of the painful moments or relationships we
prefer to keep tucked away in the hope that they will not
trouble us. Included in these things are guilts, fears, sins
and actions of which we are most ashamed.

These painful, sometimes dreaded, things of the past are
not inactive, even though we may push them out of the way.
They had their effect upon us at the time they happened
and that effect remains (though perhaps faded), even

though we may prefer to hide them away. For example, when ministering to a man, as we went over his schooldays, he remembered that he had been sexually assaulted by some older boys. He had not thought of that incident for years until it was brought to mind as we talked. As he now faced it squarely, all the old emotions of humiliation, shame, hate and desire for revenge welled up within him. They had been there unnoticed all those years and not until that moment was their release possible.

Our conscious mind has stored up within it a vast number of memories – experiences, thoughts, reactions and knowledge, of which we are, or can be, aware and over which we have a large measure of control. These go back into our past and the sum of the experiences over the years combine to make us what we are. As we have observed, some of these have been painful and we may have reacted with strong, even violent emotions such as resentment, dread, shame or rage. These, unless dealt with, will remain within us, forming our character and, if other hurtful things happen to us, we will react in the same way and the damaging emotions will gain a greater hold upon us.

Most harmful is the experience of rejection. It can come to people in many ways. A boy or girl is sometimes for some reason not accepted by others in the form or in the street in which they live. A man is passed over in the matter of promotion, or the humiliation of being snubbed can give the impression of being discarded. Someone so treated said, 'I felt as though I had been thrown on the rubbish heap.' These moments in our lives bite deeply and the effect of rejection is probably more damaging than anything else which happens to us.

It is most devastating when it occurs at the hands of our parents. If, for whatever reason, a child has not been fully accepted or wanted by his parents, the effect is bound to be serious since parents are intimately involved in the emotional condition of their children. A baby is totally dependent upon its parents who are its only source of security. If they do not provide caring, food, clothing, protection and attention, it will die. They also provide the personality of the child and the environment into which it enters and lives. During the most impressionable years of its life these factors act upon the child and have a profound effect upon its later life.

When the parents are emotionally healthy, having a loving relationship with each other and enjoy their baby, he is likely to be a happy child, active and smiling, responding to his parents. He will grow up an extrovert, making friends easily, will enjoy active things and be likely to adapt himself to people and situations.

But if the parents are in a poor emotional state because of anxiety, inner conflicts or illness, it may take them all their time to cope with their own relationships and situation. They have little of themselves to give to their child.

The sense of rejection can come to a child in a subtle way. Parents do not have to ill-treat physically or even mentally, to cause problems for their children. They can intend to be good parents, supply all needs and care for their offspring, and yet be themselves so emotionally tied-up that they are unable to express or demonstrate their love. One hears time and again, 'My parents loved me, but I hardly remember ever being kissed or cuddled.' So the one thing the child hungered for, the sure demonstration that he was loved, wanted and enjoyed, he never received. This can cause strong emotional reactions so that later he may fear to admit what he really feels about his parents through guilt of the intensity of his emotions. So he will convince himself that he feels and has always felt warmly towards his parents. The accepting of what are his true feelings can then be an extremely painful experience. An illustration of this is given under 'Conflict' later in this chapter.

Not relating to his parents will mean that a child will not develop the ability to relate to people generally unless help is given. He will tend to go into himself, build a little world of his own within and become self-conscious, sensitive, hesitant, even fearful. Within him may smoulder terror, rage, hopelessness and hate. These emotions can be produced within the baby from the first days of its life. The baby will not, of course, be aware of them. They are an automatic response to conditions which are disturbing and distressing. They will be thrust by him into the unconscious and he will have been severely damaged. The result will be that he will develop into an adult with emotional problems which will plague his life and may end in mental illness unless dealt with.

The unconscious mind

The part of our personality which registers experiences beyond our immediate awareness is called the unconscious. Despite its being hidden, it has a profound effect upon our lives. It may well contain influences from generations past as well as what comes directly from our parents and others. Each person also forms the unconscious by his reactions to what happens to him during life. This includes sending into it certain experiences which are too painful to bear. They so disturb or terrify us that we cannot bear to keep them as a conscious memory. We have then to send them into the unconscious and hope that they will not cause us bother.

We do this either by what is called 'suppression' or 'repression'. Suppression means that it is a conscious action on our part. We quite deliberately push an experience out of the way. Repression is an unconscious action. That is to say, some things cause such intense hurt that they are immediately thrust into the unconscious as a reflex action, so that we live as though they have never happened. For example, a parent may disappoint a child deeply over some matter. The child, however, so badly needs to feel secure in his parents that he will repress the incident immediately in order to keep his trust in the parent alive. This process of repression commences at birth.

Since distressing things are driven down, the person concerned will fear to have them brought to the surface. He will fear not only the painful incident or state but also the violent emotions and griefs which accompany them.

Christ can be brought into these dark, hidden areas and He is able to work a release which brings healing and joy. The healing of the memories is concerned with this. It is to be led by the Spirit to the areas of suffering, conscious and unconscious, and then by prayer to bring Christ Jesus into them, so that He may remove the hurt, deal with the emotions generated and heal.

Conflict

Problems come to us when the conscious and the unconscious are in conflict. The conscious mind wants to go one way, and the unconscious resists. A person can be torn into two and not know why. He is mystified because he seems to lose control of himself. He wants to get on with life and work but cannot cope. He has gone to pieces. So he gets depressed, fast loses confidence in himself and feels ashamed and a failure. The worst of it is that he does not know why, and no matter how hard he tries the situation does not improve. It is rather like walking in a cloud, with nothing to grasp. The reason for this state is that he is unaware of powerful forces operating within him. The fact that they have been pushed down or forgotten does not in any·way lessen their effect. It is likely that the reverse is true.

We may give an example. A young woman is on tranquillisers. She feels rejected, inadequate and depressed. She is unable to get down to work. She is constantly on the verge of tears. After some enquiry it is found that deep down she has a fear and hatred of her father. As she describes her past family life, it is clear that his character and behaviour were certainly such as would produce this reaction. As we talked together at the beginning of the interview, however, she had said, 'I loved my father.' The conflict of what she was trying to do with her conscious mind, i.e. to love her father, and what she really – but up to that time unconsciously – felt about him, caused her condition.

When she was able to realise and then face how she really felt about her father, and we prayed Christ into the past years of suffering, she was healed. At one point during the prayer she began to cry out with the voice of a little girl, 'Daddy, daddy, I want to please you. Daddy, daddy, I am so sorry. I did my best, daddy. I tried so hard to do my best. Oh, daddy, thank you for not hitting me.' The agony of that girl was in those words and expressed the bottled-up torment within.

Such unrealised pain of the past cannot be dealt with by human action alone. We are grateful to psychiatry for teaching us about the human personality and for techniques to help distressed minds. But even if we are helped to realise the seat of the problem, the psychiatrist cannot heal, though understanding of the cause of mental suffering and a warm, sensitive attitude can alleviate the pain. The young lady had been under medical care, including that of a psychiatrist. It was the Holy Spirit's discerning of the cause of the distress and our Lord's action within her which produced the healing. God alone is able to enter the unconscious as well as the conscious mind. When He is taken within them, He works to release, forgive and heal.

Though damaging experiences can come to us at any time of our life, there are certain stages when we are particularly vulnerable. In the ministry of healing of past hurts it is helpful to be aware of these. We will mention them briefly, concentrating on the earlier ones.

The unconscious houses sensations and experiences which go back to our conception. While the foetus is developing within the womb it is sensitive to the emotional state of the mother. This has an effect upon the child at a formative time, and may be the source of future distress should the mother during pregnancy be under strain or in an unhappy state of mind.

The process of birth itself can have a profound effect upon the child. Paul Tournier has described this in his book *What's in a Name?*:

An indissoluble bond is ... established between mother and child before the birth, in that happy period during which nothing separates him from his mother, when he is aware only of soft and muffled sounds, when he is wrapped in warmth, and without doing anything himself he receives food and oxygen, where he can perform tricks like a cosmonaut in a state of weightlessness. It is hardly surprising that so many people, like me, are lazy all their lives, after such an easy start.

With birth, all is changed. Our first contact with the world outside is brutal. The cold, the light, the noise and commotion, the lack of oxygen, the hands of the midwife manipulating the child, sometimes the forceps, the fall into a void, the separation from the mother – everything conspires to make this first turning-point in our lives traumatic. It is noteworthy that one of the earliest psychoanalysts, Rank, suspected that behind all our anxieties, and making us sensitive to them, lies this primitive anxiety experienced at birth.

If the birth goes well, nevertheless, it is a liberating and positive experience for the baby. It is born to live and it naturally co-operates in its entry into the world. However, the baby may be trapped for a long period within the pelvis and this may cause terror. Should he have to fight for a long time to get out, it may result in his wishing to give up the struggle and to slide back into the womb. Thus the birth process may be the source of a later dispirited attitude towards life. The pain and trauma of being crushed as he passes through the pelvic girdle can leave a lasting imprint upon the baby. Dr Frank Lake, who has done much work in this field, has demonstrated that an adult is able to re-enact his birth. This can be a remarkable experience and a releasing one as the early suffering is brought to consciousness. This is again referred to in chapter ten.

The shock of entry into the world, as described by Dr. Tournier, is clearly a vital moment in the life of the child. Suddenly, quite alone and unprotected, it is in urgent need of the comfort of its mother's arms. If, for any reason, it is left for a period unattended, this can seriously affect its future ability to relate to its mother. One girl was, after birth in hospital, separated from her mother for three weeks. The effect of rejection, self-abnegation and of feeling unlovable had a devastating result upon her adult life. The medical profession is giving attention to this important moment in life, and a new approach is being advocated in certain quarters which should help to give the unborn child the security of love which it requires. Such an approach is described in *Birth Without Violence* by Frederick Leboyer (Wildwood House Press).

A baby cannot screen himself from the atmosphere which he enters. The actual state of the parents and the home are directly impressed. If there is anxiety in the mother or if the relationship between mother and father is poor, this will be communicated to the baby. A baby is utterly dependent on its parents. His one great need is the security which only love can give. If, for some reason, this is denied or appears to be denied, then there will be disturbance within him. Any sense of rejection, lack of love, being left unattended or underfed can cause fear. This may powerfully affect his future life, driving him into himself and leading to later problems. These early days of life can be a period where there is real need of healing.

As the child grows, he becomes aware of his father. So far he has been aware only of his mother, his source of life. He then discovers someone else who has a place in his mother's affection. The father becomes a challenge to the baby. There can come the fear that the father will take the mother from him, but there is also the need of a father and the baby will be wanting to respond to him. If the father takes on his true role of affection and 'maleness', with the security and enrichment of life that this will bring, then his entry into the child's consciousness will fulfil further needs in the baby's development. Should this not be the case, the child will be forced to face a contest for which he is unequipped.

The question of authority is clearly involved here. Parents are normally the people who give a child his first impression of authority. If they are firm, loving and consistent, the child knows what is allowed and what is expected of him and has a stable framework of behaviour. He can learn that love and discipline go together, that the acceptance of proper authority gives security and happiness, and this will lead him into self-discipline. If the authority is weak or indulgent, the child will resent this, for decisions are put upon him too early and security is denied him. Similarly the child is ill-equipped to respond to an authority which is possessive or over-demanding; where it is so heavy as to crush, or where it is changeable – strong one moment and indulgent at another.

School, of course, contributes to a child's conception of authority. It means for him an adjustment to a different form of authority in differing circumstances. But school is more than this. It requires an adjustment to a situation which a child must make alone. He has to stand alone, probably for the first time, in a world which may suddenly have become unfriendly and where he is not the apple of everyone's eye. The cruelty of children to each other is proverbial and he is forced to measure up to this. He may be able to take this as a challenge and in that case he will benefit, but for many a child this has been a frightening time. Pressure from parents and teachers for academic progress and fear of failure may also later have its effect upon the child. One has, in addition, had to deal with the devastating consequence of the attitude of some masters and mistresses to particular children under their control.

As he grows into adolescence a whole new crop of forces come into play physically and emotionally. New horizons, opportunities and desires open up and, with these, the demands and adjustments which they bring. Often it seems that with the abounding energy many adolescents show, the strain and adjustments which come to them are not appreciated. Since, at this stage, they can often become inarticulate, they have to bear their problems alone. The present-day attitude towards sex does not make it any easier for them to handle this explosive instinct. On the contrary, the absence of control, the freedom for experiment and the lack of public opinion and guidelines often leave them lost. Many young people express their resentment at this, and it can augur ill for their marriage.

These stages, with their entry into the world of work, will have a profound effect upon development and can bring pain, problems and damaging experiences which, if not healed, will make life a burden. For reasons they cannot discover, people feel bewildered, unwanted, haunted by fear, anxiety and guilt, depressed and hopeless as a result of the past. If we can enter understandingly and sensitively into their life, the Holy Spirit will help us to know those points which are the source of such suffering.

We cannot truly enter into the sorrows, pains and humiliations of others without having ourselves gone through some such suffering. We have to work through our own pains by going to others 'to open our grief'. If we are not prepared to do this because of pride or fear, we will have little chance of rapport with others in their suffering, nor indeed will we be the type of person to whom they feel they can open their hearts. We cannot lead others where we have not been. Further, if we have been unwilling to enter into our own pain, we shall not see the necessity for others to enter into theirs, nor, indeed, shall we be able to show them how this is possible.

The reason Christ can enter our sufferings and lead us to share those of others is that He felt human pain without reserve in His own flesh. 'For we have not a high priest who is unable to sympathise with our weaknesses, but one who in every respect has been tempted as we are, yet without sinning. . . . In the days of his flesh, Jesus offered up prayers and supplications, with loud cries and tears, to him who was able to save him from death, and he was heard for his godly fear. Although he was a Son, he learned obedience through what he suffered. . . . Let us then with confidence draw near to the throne of grace, that we may receive mercy and find grace to help in time of need' (Heb. 4:15, 5:7–8, 4:16).

When *we* have suffered in our flesh, we can know what it is to stay and share with others as they agonise 'with loud cries and tears' in re-living their dread, desolation, rage and confusion. As the Holy Spirit brings the painful to consciousness, we can help them to let Christ Jesus enter into it and act to heal.

9

Some results of disorder

Those who suffer as a result of inner conflict will show evidence of it. Some of these features we will now mention, since anyone who takes part in the ministry of healing of past sufferings will be bound to meet them.

First we should say that people with deep emotional problems might be expected to be in a more distressed condition than those who require only a listening ear. This may be the case, but appearances can be deceptive. A well-controlled exterior may cover a deeper need than exists in an emotional kind of person.

Those who require healing of the memories will particularly feel insecure and rejected. They will very likely be perplexed and discouraged because all their own (and perhaps other people's) efforts to 'shake out of it' have failed. We may not find them logical in thinking or expression, and should that be so, it will require patience to piece together a coherent story to find the cause. Some find it hard to talk, others are quite the reverse.

Whatever their condition or attitude, they must be accepted unconditionally for themselves. Warm, genuine acceptance is the way to help them to be at ease and to speak of themselves as well as to be themselves. Many do not feel that they are themselves but are what others have made them. The healing of our Lord will give them a sense of worth, free them from themselves, and make them able to stand on their own feet with more trust in Him.

In establishing relationships with people who feel inadequate our attitude should be natural and encouraging. We should treat them with the dignity of giving them our full attention and receive what they say thoughtfully and with serious consideration. To dismiss their words lightly or to contradict or disagree in any hasty manner will immediately drive them into their insecurity and effectively terminate hope of further progress.

Very likely they will find it difficult to speak of their family, of their painful experiences or of their intimate thoughts and reactions. They are often ashamed of what they are and feel, and some assume that they are un-lovable. When they do gain confidence to speak it must be received sensitively and courteously. A man whose self-revelation had been treated lightly said, 'I felt as though he had spat in my face.'

If, however, they feel that they truly matter to us, that we are doing our best to understand them and long for them to be free, they will recognise it and respond.

As we enter into the lives of those burdened with the past, we shall almost certainly meet three conditions – guilt, fear and anxiety. These can have strong roots and only healing at depth is able to deal with them. A word about these should be given.

Guilt

Some guilt is right and should be felt. If we deliberately do what we know to be wrong, then we should feel our guilt. We need to be faced with it, repent and receive God's forgiveness. But there is other guilt which is our reaction to something *done to us*, often when we were young. For example, a person will bitterly resent her possessive mother but will be in a state of condemnation for the antagonism she feels. She is right to react against being possessed, because to be truly human we need to be free in order to develop and mature, but her mother has created a guilt by insinuating that her child is repudiating her love.

Guilts derive from the standards set by parents and others when fear of punishment or rejection colour the censure. A baby may be reprimanded, 'You dirty little boy, Mummy is cross with you,' when his motions did not fit her timetable. One man told me that as a result of such an attitude he had constipation for years. In the same way the first assertive actions or sexual explorations may be rebuffed in such a way that expression of personality and sex both become 'wrong' and infected with guilt.

Much guilt has its source in the years before a child is fully self-conscious. We are not, therefore, responsible for such things, though we may condemn ourselves for what we feel and for the way such experiences effect our adult lives. Evidence of such underlying guilt may be detected in someone who is a compulsive worker, or who over-eats or under-eats. Others may be a prey to scruple. Some by guilt are driven to be perfectionists or have an obsession for washing – they feel themselves unclean. Strong inferiority and sensitivity to criticism may also indicate underlying guilt.

To remove deep guilts, their roots have first to be exposed. As we go back into the earlier years and show some of the influences which were in a person's life, the emotions causing the guilts come to light. Being exposed, they can be expressed and so lose their power. We can help the guilty ones also to realise that many of their emotional reactions such as hate, rage or resentment were inevitable, as has already been indicated. When Christ is brought into the situation which occasioned the guilt and He releases from the suffering, a person begins to have a new attitude towards himself and is able to forgive those who were the cause of his suffering.

Fear

Just as there is healthy and unhealthy guilt, so there is good and bad fear. Fear can be a life-saver but it may also paralyse us. Many fears are conscious fears – fear of failure, ridicule, hurt, loneliness, illness, death, people and of the future.

With realised fears, we can defeat them by facing them squarely. Some who suffer in this way think that if they look at their fear, it will be indelibly printed upon their minds. The reverse is the case. Refusing to look at fears adds to their strength and haunting power. To look straight at a fear, speak to it and ask, 'What is the worst that could happen if this fear were realised?' is the way to dispel it. Many have been helped by the suggestion that they look straight at their fear and *through* the fear to Christ. Our Lord is then given the opportunity to remove it.

There are fears, however, not so manageable. They have a cause which is not remembered and the effect makes for abnormal behaviour. These are called phobias. So, for example, we meet those who are terrified of being in an enclosed place (called claustrophobia) or who cannot face being outside in the open (called agoraphobia). Some will attach their fear to an object in order to mitigate their dread. They use such things as spiders or snakes or their own bodies – and spend large amounts of money on patent medicines. Others are just fearful and do not know why.

Fears of this type are not easily dislodged. Their removal may take time. We can, however, pray for the cause to be revealed. This may come about by careful questioning regarding the past, but sometimes the Holy Spirit will show it to us. A lady complained of a dread of death. As we talked and prayed, it was revealed that there was a double cause, first that something had happened during the process of birth which had terrified her, and the other that she had at one time had contact with a fortune teller and others with psychic powers. She feared that at death her spirit would be taken by evil spirits.

It is the action of Christ who is 'perfect love and casts out fear' (1 John 4:18) which effects release. We can take Him right into the fear so that He may break its power and remove it. If the cause of the fear is known, we can pray that He will enter and deal with the situation which produced the fear. If the fear cannot be specified, or should its cause remain unknown, we may still ask our Lord to enter that part of the personality which He knows to be the seat of the trouble.

Anxiety

Fear can express itself in anxiety. Anxiety has been called by W. L. Carrington (*Psychology, Religion and Human Need* published by the Epworth Press) the 'black sheep of the family' of fear: the degradation of the essential and valuable protective mechanism of fear to the useless destructive futility of worry'. Anxiety grips a person despite all efforts to counteract it, and gnaws absorbing energy and, like strong fear, inhibiting action. It causes people to wake in the early hours of the morning. They lie in bed in a state of agitation which makes the coming day an agony of anticipation.

Anxiety has its roots deep within our personality and goes back not only to particularly stressful times which we can remember (as, for example, pressure by parents and teachers to do well), but also to times before we could express anything, as when left unattended for long periods as a baby. Something may be said or sensed in the present which touches the previous traumatic experience and we begin to be anxious. We had the case of a woman who was a twin. At birth her sister was the weaker of the two and so had the mother's attention. For some time the stronger was kept away from the mother and fed by the nursing staff. The period when she was denied the comfort and security of her mother created a terror of loneliness and insecurity. No one cared, no one came when she cried, no one loved her – that was the effect on her. The result was that, as an adult, whenever she received a letter from her mother she was gripped with anxiety. Some people live in a constant state of stress which torments their existence. When we meet anxiety, we should behave understandingly, for it can be a cause of severe suffering.

Though anxiety springs from the past, it affects our future. We feel inadequate to face life and even small things seem too demanding. Decisions are difficult and sometimes impossible to make. Anxiety seems to have its origin in insecurity of some form. Often this origin is unknown but its effect is that for seemingly no concrete reason, people are disturbed, worried, oppressed and may find it hard to concentrate. Few of us escape it altogether.

Healing of the memories is a way of getting to these insecurities of bygone days. As we explore the past, we ask the Holy Spirit to bring to light those things which have caused damage and disturbed the inner peace. To bring Christ into these exposed sufferings goes a long way to ameliorate the tension. Our Lord heals these crushing experiences and brings His caring and acceptance in their place, so creating a new seed-bed of a positive and tranquil attitude. We may take our Lord, as with fears, into the hidden areas where root causes of anxiety exist. Christ works there also, for no part of us exists of which He is ignorant.

Christ deals with the past but still, after ministry, old habits of mind can continue. If our state of stress has been severe we have, in addition, become people who dread that they may be rejected in the present and the future. After the healing of the past, in order to remove old habits of thought and to create a new attitude towards the future, it is necessary to grow in Christ in order that He may become our security. Our relationship with Him must be put on a solid and maturing basis. We must be taught how to grow in prayer and in gaining strength from the Bible.

To repeat to ourselves positive, trusting words will help create the right attitude. Our Lord's words, 'Do not be anxious for your life' with His positive application 'Seek first his kingdom and his righteousness' (Matt. 6:25,33) are obvious ones to choose as are St. Paul's in Phil. 4:6–7. We should, however, ask the Spirit to indicate to us words which will be particularly appropriate to our own personality. The prayer of Teresa of Avila has inspired many to find the trust in Christ which dispels anxiety. 'Let nothing disturb thee, nothing affright thee; all things are passing; God never changeth. Patient endurance attaineth to all things; whom God possesseth in nothing is wanting: alone God sufficeth.'

However, it is the basic process of losing our present life to find the life of Christ which is the final healing. As we become less self-concerned, so we have less about which to be worried. Anxiety is usually obsession with ourselves. As we, under God's hand, change and like a grain of wheat die to ourselves, He produces a different growth (John 12:24–6).

Our Lord followed these words by immediately demonstrating their aptness in His own life. The cross is looming ahead, but He is not torn by anxious foreboding, though He is about to suffer utter rejection by 'his own'. At that moment, as always, His concentration is solely upon doing His Father's will. 'Now is my soul troubled. And what shall I say? "Father, save me from this hour?" No, for this purpose I have come to this hour. Father, glorify thy name.' (John 12:27–8). As the Holy Spirit leads us into this same unawareness of ourselves, so anxiety loses its hold.

Relationship with God

In thinking of the state of mind of those seeking healing, it may be profitable to mention one or two matters regarding their relationship with God.

As the healing of the past is the work of Christ, there must be active and willing co-operation with Him on the part of those who come for help. It is therefore essential that their relationship with God be sorted out. This will necessitate a real relationship between the two parties, and this forms the basis from which ministry can progress.

It sometimes requires gentle and sensitive questioning to draw out what people feel about God. If their attitude to Him is anything but cordial they may find it difficult to admit this to themselves, let alone anyone else. It may help in such a case to point out (a) God sees them as they actually are, resentment and all, and so there is no point in attempting to appear other than we are. Bible passages such as

Ps. 139:1–18 or Luke 12:6–7 may help. (b) We may need to insist that we are in no way judging them, only trying to find out their true situation. We may have to make it clear that we cannot minister unless they are willing to be real about themselves. (c) It may ease them when they realise that much antagonism towards God dates from our earliest months and years. Our responses then were unconscious and so not culpable. If we have ourselves felt attitudes towards God similar to their own and have learnt to come to Him, finding His acceptance and forgiveness, the sharing of this may be beneficial.

It is natural for us to make God in the image of our earliest dominant authority. This normally is our parents. When we, as little children pray 'Our Father', we automatically think of our heavenly Father in terms of our earthly one. He colours our idea of God. If the parent is warm, affectionate and stable, the child will have no difficulty in his approach to God. If, however, the parent is distant, unloving, feared, then God will be seen in a similar way, and there will be a reaction against Him.

In addition, our experience of people and of life moulds our characters. We may become gentle, compassionate as we react, or angry, resentful and fearful. If certain things are said or done which cause a recollection, conscious or unconscious, of areas of past hurt, we will react according to the person we have become. This will be so with God for we cannot but be what we are, no matter who is at the other end. A resentful person will be resentful towards God, as he is resentful towards people.

Many do not at first accept this. They complain, 'I cannot feel God's presence when I pray.' What is happening is that (as described in chapter eight) they are to some extent two people. Their conscious desire is for God, but as they move in spirit towards Him, the part which is antagonistic draws away from Him, and that unconscious part is the stronger force. So for all their effort they do not make contact with God. They are bewildered and frustrated. When they are made aware of what is happening within them, they are able to bring their antagonism as well as their desire to God, knowing that He will accept them as they are.

It has been found that the fact of God having revealed Himself to us as Trinity also provides a way through the deadlock of enmity towards God. When people are 'anti-God' for any reason, it usually appears that they are thinking in terms of the Father. They divide the Trinity in that they can be antagonistic towards God (the Father) but are able to love Jesus whom they know from the Gospels loves them and died for them.

Though this is inadmissible from a theological point of view, it is common experience. It is easier for most people to regard God as Trinity rather than as One. We can use this in a situation where only God is able to heal, but where there is resistance to Him. Experience shows that from an emotional standpoint, a person is able to take Jesus into himself, even though opposed to God the Father. Our Lord can do His healing work, even to the point of dealing with the wrong emotional attitude towards the Father. After being freed, the day will come when the love of the Father will be seen and accepted just as is that of the Son. So within the understanding and experience of such a person the Godhead is unified.

An experience at the beginning of life may cause an inability later on to feel the presence of God. One person was in this state into middle age. As she was being ministered to, it became clear that during the period immediately after birth, she had been left unattended for a considerable time. In ministry she re-lived the dread of feeling 'nothing was there'. That is, she lived through once again the period when, as a baby, she cried and cried but no one came and how she had felt utterly alone, unwanted, desperate. As she re-experienced this she was freed from the fear that 'no one is there', and was able to receive the Lord into that agonising vacuum. Since then she has known the presence of God.

A result of disorder is the reliance on drugs. While these make it possible for people to carry on when otherwise life would be too heavy a burden, and while drugs can correct chemical imbalance, dependence on them for many offends their self-respect. We touch on this subject only as it may affect emotional healing.

Harm has been done by ill-advised action. There have been cases where drugs have been thrown away immediately after prayer when no word came from the Spirit. This has caused serious consequences to their condition as well as to their relationship with their doctor. I have known those who after prayer have been so sure that our Lord has healed, that they have ceased to take their drugs with no ill-effects. As a general rule, however, the doctor should be consulted. In my experience the body or mind of a person for whom prayer was made has indicated after a time that drugs could be reduced or dispensed with. Consultation with the doctor has followed. I believe that in such cases it was the Spirit indicating the progress of the healing.

10

The healing of the past

If we are to release anyone from suffering caused by the past, we need to bring to light under the Spirit's guidance the experiences which caused the pain. People vary in their approach to this ministry. Some prefer to work alone with the one in distress because they believe that a closer and more trusting relationship can develop, with only one personal adjustment to be made by the needy person.

Others choose to work with one or two others. This means that the prayer and experience of more than one person is available and all present can be open to the Holy Spirit as He speaks and directs. It can also lessen the emotional dependence upon the helper. In this case one will take the lead, the others praying, waiting on God, observing and commenting where it is necessary. We should not overlook the value of a man and woman ministering together. Each sex has its own distinctive insights into character and can contribute to understanding and fulfilment.

Group work is effective and is becoming popular. The members of the group as a body become the recipients of God's love and those to whom ministry is being given respond to the love and caring of the group. Groups are useful for those who find it difficult to ask for help personally. By being members of the group they are encouraged as they see others released. Such groups require an experienced leader. For those who feel led to take part in this ministry, it is clearly to their advantage to commence by being with such a group. They are able to observe and learn not only techniques, but, under the Holy Spirit, to learn to be compassionate.

Rapport with the person in need

In this ministry an important element is assisting people to express themselves, for we need to know their story. First of all those requiring help should be put at their ease. Often they are self-conscious. They must be encouraged to talk and, as they do, we can show by our attitude that we wish to enter and share their problems. If our attitude is genuine they will know and a good relationship will develop.

We need to explain clearly what we intend to do, and point out step by step what this is. We can list these steps as follows:

1. The past is causing the present difficulty.
2. Our object, therefore, is to find out what has happened in the past.
3. This means we will touch on some painful areas, but now they can be shared with us and above all with Christ.
4. We are going to ask the Holy Spirit to open up their life, especially the distressing parts, but we are bringing such events to remembrance only to make it possible for healing to take place.
5. After finding out what has happened in the past, we shall lay hands on their head or shoulders and pray through the times when pain was experienced. We shall ask the Lord Jesus to enter into each painful place, one by one, to

release the buried emotions and heal the raw wounds. He may need to grant forgiveness.

6. We may also have to cut the emotional cords which still may hold them bound to certain people, for example, a parent.

It is not easy for some to accept that the past is causing the present trouble. We need patience and careful demonstration to help them realise that the present contains the event which has sparked off their distress; that distress is there because the present has disturbed underlying conflicts. With one person it was necessary to explain the situation described in chapter eight three times. Finally it was realised that the reason for his non-acceptance was that he thought we were criticising his parents. We had to make it clear that all we were after were the *facts* of his relationship and the result of it. When parents dominate a child they often inculcate a false loyalty. This causes guilt when the relationship is examined.

Having accepted that the past is the problem, it is not easy for many to face distressing memories. They would rather keep them out of sight. We have to help them to understand that the way to release is precisely the opposite. When we allow ourselves to face and feel the emotional pain in the love and power of Christ, its grip on us is broken and it can be used constructively to mellow and mature. We commonly meet those who are not able to allow the pain to be brought out because in earlier years they were not permitted to express themselves. The 'stiff upper lip' has caused many to become almost incapable of normal self-expression. I lived next door to a Scottish family. Whenever the children were in trouble or had hurt themselves they were told, 'Scots people do not cry.'

The result of such situations is that a solid blockage is constructed which shuts off the areas needing release and healing. This blockage has to be removed. As we point this out, we may say something like this: 'Christ has seen your suffering, every bit of it from birth, and He has suffered with you. Now, if you will go back to it and feel it again, He can let you know how He has suffered for you and will now suffer with you. Let us take Him into the cold-shut-off parts within to bring His warmth, His loving acceptance, and His healing.'

Those who minister have the privilege of assisting people to do this by staying with them as they move into the painful times. We can patiently encourage them not to be afraid, and gently but firmly prevent them from turning away from the pain. I will quote part of a letter from someone who faced her true self and situation. It was her second visit. Previously we had been able to open up her relationship with her mother. This letter describes her trepidation as she prepared to come the second time and the result of being helped to face her pain.

On the Monday last week I sat in the car park just outside ... for ages and just could not drive on down the hill, and if it had not been late afternoon I think I would have turned round and gone home! I am so glad I did not, though Wednesday and Thursday after our first talk were pretty miserable ones and I have never felt so awful – and I have had some very low periods too. I was just so very cold all over with an icy lump in my middle and the general feeling of being kicked. I was really afraid when I came to you on Thursday evening – after you had prayed with me I went to bed still feeling very cold and after what seemed hours a gentle warmth began to flow through me and then it became quite intense and I fell asleep. This strong heat was there when I woke up and stayed that way for about an hour – with a real presence of the Lord which I have never experienced before – the rash had gone too. Bless and thank you for entering into that with me – alone I could never have faced all my deep anger, resentment and bitterness and the knowledge that I really did want to do away with my mother. I just had not realised this deep anger etc. was strong in me and I am so glad that you made me face up to this – painful as it was. It is good not to feel condemned now.

It is for this reality and release that we are working in the healing of the past. A good rapport must therefore be established so that deep things (and often to the sufferer, shameful things) are exposed and dealt with.

Going into past history

When we go into the past, we must obviously obtain information mainly from the one in trouble. There are some things which we should have in mind.

Are we allowing him to tell his story in his own way? This can sometimes be irritating, for he may be under stress or vague and wandering as he talks about his life and how he feels or felt. As he speaks we try to piece together his story, listening carefully to him and asking the Holy Spirit to indicate conflict areas so that later we do not waste time on unimportant things. We try to note what he omits or glosses over.

Do we use the way he talks about himself to gain an insight into his emotional condition and how he reacted to the situations of his life? If we are to do this, he must be permitted to tell his story unhurriedly.

Are we tempted to evaluate his experience in terms of our

own? This is a common weakness. We need to realise the individuality of each person. No two of us will react in an identical way to the same situation. We must endeavour to enter into his mind and heart, learning to say with Ezekiel, 'I sat where they sat'. In other words, we should try to understand what it is like *to be him*.

It is not wise to ask questions early in the conversation unless to clarify some point or check some detail. Let him speak, for sometimes as he does he will become aware of things he had not realised previously. When he is describing his life, we may become confused by the mass of detail and presentation, but let him continue for as long as he desires. We can trust the Spirit to discern for us the things that will need special attention. As the Spirit does this, the whole story will take shape and we shall be able to pray confidently when the time comes.

After he has finished his story we may talk about it to underline the important things that have happened to him or of which he has been deprived, explaining the effect of these upon him. We should take nothing for granted for he will be, as we all are, blind to much of himself. When we question, we do so in order to bring out the full implication of the salient features and to show him things which he had been unable to realise before. We aim to show him to himself together with the significance of what has happened to him and been the cause of inner pain.

In chapter eight we listed some of the times in our lives when we are vulnerable to emotional injury. We should be careful to note what is said about these periods and particularly to enquire about the state of relationships within them. We should find out what sort of relationship existed between the parents, as well as his own relationship with father, mother, step-parent or guardian and the rest of the family. We should note in what order he came among the children and if others followed soon after. If they did, he is likely to have been pushed aside so that the mother's attention could be given to the later arrival. The happenings within the family during his earlier years are also important, such as absence of a parent or parents because of work, divorce or separation. Illnesses, deaths, tragedies are significant, particularly if they caused the loss of a secure relationship or brought about fear or anxiety.

As we work through his life we shall recognise when distress was caused and emotional injury incurred. It may help to note these so that they are in our minds when the time comes to pray them through. Though exploring the past may take an appreciable amount of time, when the moment arrives to pray it through, we find that our Lord so often performs a work of healing in a short time.

Praying for healing

We may now indicate a method of praying through the past. For the sake of clarity we again list the steps:

1. All concerned should place themselves under the Holy Spirit so that, for the whole operation, they may be sensitive to Him.
2. The one who is to pray through the past may stand behind the person to whom ministry is being given, laying hands on head or shoulders.
3. Then, under the Holy Spirit, he should pray back into the past, taking each period at a time and, within it, any particular traumatic experience e.g. the baby's entry into the world. It seems natural to start from the beginnings of life, but on occasion it is better to commence with later suffering. The Spirit will indicate.
4. In the prayer we go over in word and spirit the circum-stances surrounding and the factors involved in each

period of life. We ask the one being ministered to to enter into and re-live past happenings as far as he is able. He should tell the person praying anything which is recalled so that this is also taken into the prayer for healing.

5. For the earliest periods we need particularly to be attentive to the Spirit as these cover times before consciousness. He may give a vision or word of knowledge which will indicate pertinent factors. As the early period is pre-verbal, only God can reveal such times or even be aware of them. So the one being prayed for should be encouraged to let Him enter these areas of unconscious experience.

6. As we pray, we ask the Spirit to open up the roots of suffering, including fears, anxieties, guilts and deeply buried emotions.

7. As the Spirit opens up each period, we ask Jesus to enter into it – both the situation and the pain. We should already have led him to feel again the pain of that time. Now Jesus is brought right into it to heal. There may be hurts still locked in the unconscious and so we pray also for our Lord to open these doors, to enter and to heal. There may be a strong reaction as release comes.

8. Our Lord will heal the raw wounds of each period. We allow time for Him to move within and bring peace at each stage, not going on to the next stage until this happens.

9. As we pray through, so we have to bring Jesus into the suffering caused by wrong or poor relationships. We have already said that the most distressing relationship is likely to be parental. The person concerned may still be bound emotionally to his parents, even though one or both are dead. We can, by the Spirit's authority, cut

the emotional cords which hold him to his parents, using such words as, 'In the Name and by the power and authority of the Holy Spirit I cut you free from any ties which still subject you to your parent(s).' It has been found helpful to ask the person so freed to imagine that his parents are sitting before him. He can then 'see' them from his new freedom and the way is open for him to forgive and pray for them.

The prayer for healing

It may be of assistance if an actual prayer for the healing of the memories is given. The form and content of such a prayer will, naturally, vary with the person making it. We should not attempt to copy others. In her book *Healing Gifts of the Spirit* Agnes Sanford has written the kind of prayer she would offer to the Lord. It may be compared with the following prayer I might be likely to pray. Jim is a fictitious character.

Dear Lord, we bless You that we are in Your presence and that You know all there is to be known of your servant Jim. We thankfully remember that Your love is not only infinite but is able to meet all our needs, so we come to You knowing that You will richly bless and work as we pray.

We ask You, Holy Spirit, to open up the very springs of Jim's life back to his conception, so that Christ Jesus may enter to touch with His healing hand.

We go back, dear Lord, to the early months of Jim's life as he was within his mother. Since we realise, Lord, that she was then in an unhappy and fearful state, we ask You to remove from Jim whatever may have affected him adversely. Enter right into any fear that may remain there, take it from him and in its place put Your healing peace and joy, with Your desire that Jim should embrace and savour life. . . .

As we pray for his birth, Lord, I feel a strong awareness that this was protracted and painful. We ask You to heal the wounds caused by those hours of suffering. Take away the unwillingness to live which Jim felt and replace it with Your glorious life. . . .

Our heart aches, Lord, as we think of Jim's entry into the world. We pray for Your healing touch upon him as he entered a situation where his parents were estranged; his father unfaithful and his mother broken-hearted. Dear Lord, enter into that cold, unloving atmosphere which Jim assimilated. Come with Your warm, welcoming love and joy into that cold, grey area within him, where rejection, rage and bitterness have formed and make it all new with Your glorious life and hope. . . .

So we may pray through each period of Jim's life where suffering had come. Finally we ask God's forgiveness for any pain Jim may himself have caused others by retaliation. Then we commend him into the hands of Christ.

The full release from the past may not always come with the first prayer. One reason is that some people are so hurt, and have become so enclosed in themselves, that they dare not open themselves all at once. Thus the first prayer may heal only a part of their sufferings. In other cases the hurts cannot heal immediately because the one injured is not yet able to forgive and still nurses bitterness and a desire for revenge. It also happens that some bitter experiences come back to mind subsequent to prayer having been made. We may, therefore, see a person more than once, each prayer bringing more release, healing and confidence.

He can do much himself. In his daily prayer he may take our Lord into the same areas for which prayer has been made and so allow Him to continue His healing. If he will open himself fully to our Lord, this will permit Christ to work in those parts which remain untouched. In any case, it is advisable that those who have been healed should take Christ regularly into every part of their being, for there is need not only for healing of the past but also to mature under God's hands.

At times, one can be called upon for 'crisis' ministry. That is, when someone comes in distress, and there is little time for ministry. In such cases Christ will do sufficient to enable the person to carry on until further help is available. We need to quieten such a person as far as we are able, praying God's peace into him and encouraging him to open his whole being to the Lord. We then lay hands, asking Christ to enter into the cause of the distress of which He is perfectly aware and to bring healing and peace. On one occasion a lady who had had not only an insecure but also a reprobate past was in great distress. After a short prayer for quietness, hands were laid on her and our Lord asked to do whatever He knew to be necessary. She received a release almost immediately with the assurance that her past was forgiven.

The same principles that have been described may be applied by people themselves in any hurt or humiliation which may happen subsequently. They should ask Christ to enter the experience, to take from them the distress and to heal the wound. This may be necessary when a person is still in close contact with another responsible for past hurts. In such instances it should be realised that habits, attitudes and memories do not disappear immediately and old sores can be re-opened. Should such a thing happen, prayer must be made at once before antagonism grows. However, when there has been full healing of the past, the attitude of the injured person is so changed that relationships from then on have a more constructive quality.

Here is part of a letter received from a lady who had had ministry four or five times. She describes how she is now able to react positively towards incidents which would previously have brought her low. With the letter she enclosed a drawing she had made to express her release by Christ. In the centre a bold cross, flaming with light, is poised triumphantly over a dark pit. A black chain which has been snapped in two lies at the foot of the cross over the pit. From a blue sky a white dove swoops over the whole scene.

When I was praying the other morning and thinking about things the enclosed picture came to me and though I am not an artist I felt I just had to try and put it on paper – it is very much my experience with the black abyss I was in, and the chain of fear, anger and rejection that the Lord has now broken, with the glory beyond the Cross for the future and the Holy Spirit revealing the Lord and His glory to me. Life has been also so grey and one long deep trough up till now and suddenly it is all different. There are peaks and being born anew – a coming to life inside me. Having pushed every emotion down inside me and not allowed myself to feel anything but pain and anger, I find the coming to life has its painful side too, even in the joy and peace which is coming to me, but the pain is different because it is one of life and not of death. God's words to me on the way home that He loves me are being borne out in so many little ways that I *know* He loves me.

During the past week there have been one or two incidents where I have felt rejected and whereas before I would have pushed all down inside and at the same time mentally rushed round in circles in panic looking for, and mostly not able to find, a re-establishment of relationships, it seemed as if Jesus was keeping every possible chance of this out of my way until I found that He was in this rejection. He has made me see that He was in that rejection, He had taken it on Himself and that here and now my acceptance, security and all that I need are in Him only. I was able to find this and to know that all along the way in these dark years He has been there all the time, and I have sensed a real healing beginning to take place.

Recently work has been done in the use of deep breathing for release of the hurts of the earliest periods of life. When this method is used, the person is asked to lie on his back on the floor, bed or couch. If on the floor place under him a thick rug or some cushions. He is first helped to relax physically and mentally so that he may come to a state of peace. It is worth giving some time to this. When relaxed, he should begin to breathe strongly and deeply, taking air into the whole area of the lungs. As he moves into the rhythm of this, he is asked to breathe Christ into the heart of his being; into the cold, shut-off areas within. After a time the baby or child of the past will begin to express itself. He may begin to sob or to make noises or speak as he did when a baby or very young. He may express, for example, the dread of being deserted in the first few hours of life. He should be allowed to continue for as long as the trauma is felt.

In many cases indications are given which point to the actual birth experience. He may feel crushed or put his hands to his head as if in pain. If so, he may be placed in the position of being within the womb (if he has not already assumed this attitude), knees up to chin and arms folded. One of those taking him through this process should kneel at his head with the man's head cupped in his hands to represent the pelvis. Another places himself at the other end to simulate the contractions of the mother. Though conscious, the actual birth can be re-enacted. If the birth was a difficult one, a great release comes as the pains and fears are worked through. The origin of the death-wish can be seen here in some instances, for the baby may have been held for so long in the pelvis, unable to move, that it wishes to give up the struggle to be born and return to the comfort and darkness of the womb.

Following this, the first few hours of life can be immediately re-lived. If the birth was difficult, it is likely that the baby was left unattended while interest was centred on the condition of the mother. In such instances, the baby could suffer a strong sense of loneliness and terror. Such a painful time can also be re-lived. As the man allows himself to relapse back to those early hours, the baby within will express the agony it then felt. This can mean the release from later suffering which had its source in those early hours of life. We have already quoted the case of the lady who, because of what happened during those hours, for years had no sense of the presence of God.

It should be said that nothing but deep breathing and prayer is used in this method. There is no state of trance, no hypnotism, no drugs.

The healing of past suffering is the work of Christ within and whenever He is brought into it benefit is received. It must not, however, be forgotten that longer-term counselling may be required by many before they are finally free from their emotional problems. If, therefore, praying through the past does not produce enough release to enable a person to come to grips with life, he should be advised to consult someone who is in a position to assist at a deeper level. All of us should have the humility to realise when we have come to the end of our own resources and the need to pass someone on to a more experienced person.

For those who wish to study Christian counselling further, information is given at the end of this book on training courses, conferences and books. Groups in churches may wish to study such books together.

II

Chain re-action

In March 1976 the Rev. John Gunstone went to Canada to lead a mission. A lady – let us call her Ann – attended one of his meetings. She was a member of a church named after St. Barnabas, and as she listened she felt that one day she would like to visit 'this place he came from' in England, also associated with Barnabas. Her husband's occupation involved him in much travelling. While sitting in her kitchen after hearing John speak, she believed that God was saying, 'Go with William on his next trip to England.' This seemed an impossibility, as his next trip was in a few days' time and she had two small children. However, all difficulties were removed.

In England she found her way to our house in Dorset. She intended simply to meet us and learn something of our life as a community. However, when talking with Lucia, she suddenly broke down and began to sob. As my wife ministered to her, the Spirit led them back to the earliest times of Ann's life. Lying on the floor she began to shake uncontrollably and to shiver, her teeth chattering. Soon she curled her body up as if in the womb and so she was taken through her birth in a manner similar to that described in the previous chapter. It was a harrowing experience and afterwards she felt a continual desire to vomit. Eventually this passed, and was followed by a deep peace. She shared her past life and problems with Lucia who counselled her for a long time.

Since she was now physically and emotionally exhausted, she was left to rest for a few hours and it was intended that she should stay the night. When the evening meal was taken to her, she had changed. She wept for joy and was radiant. She said she ought to leave after the meal and join her husband in London. Some days later we received a letter describing what happened as a result of her visit. This is what she wrote:

So much has happened in the two short weeks since I was with you. I praise and thank God every day for His love and your devotion to Him through your ministries at Whatcombe House, that have given two more individuals new lives in Christ.

Once I got on the train to London, all the happenings and revelations of the day simply overwhelmed me, and I was so thankful to have a small compartment to myself. The tears were ones of sadness and yet relief – relief to know who I really was, now free to be God's person, not a conglomeration of someone else's fears and frustrations. I guess it was then that my thoughts turned to my husband William, and I prayed that God would direct me if I was to share all that had happened with him. It was while praying about this, that I was given insight into what was binding up William in his life with his family, his job, and his progression towards God. It was an overwhelming 'fear of failure to meet expectations' that others had of him. I can remember praying that God would show me more, that perhaps William could be healed also, if this was his problem and what, if anything, I could help God with in His mission of healing.

One of the many unexpected and poignantly beautiful

experiences I've had since being with you, happened only moments later. I had to change trains at Basingstoke to get on the Reading train, and sat with a young couple who were very active in the Girl Guide movement in Britain, and who had been to a conference that day, to exchange badges from all over the world. They were very friendly and excited over their day's 'swapping' and were showing me a great suitcase of velvet-mounted badges. All of a sudden, the husband reached into his case and handed me a beautiful bronze pin. 'Here,' he said, 'I'd like you to have this pin to keep – it is called a "*Promise Pin*".'

As I sat there stunned, the word *promise* echoed in my ears, and it seemed to me that God had moved him to give me that pin as a constant reminder to me of the covenant that I have with Him, but also of His promise of healing for my darling. Almost immediately, some of the sadness round my heart seemed to leave, and that quest of 'the promise' was instilled in its place.

I was so glad to have returned to the hotel that evening, as the conference had progressed splendidly and was finished ahead of schedule, which meant William and I had Sunday all to ourselves. (This was the second unexpected occurrence.) When we were in bed that night William asked why I had been crying, since he can always tell right away. I couldn't lie about a miracle and not share the most beautiful happening of my life with the very person I shared everything else in life, so I related the story. He simply lay there, his eyes brimming with tears and at the end asked, 'Do you think God would give me a new life, too? I don't think I can go on living this one much longer!' (I must tell you that William's doctor told him a year and a half ago that he had hypertension and would have to take medication for the rest of his life.) He then went on to tell me how the meeting had been very difficult with many contentious issues, and as the moderator, they looked to him the whole time for solutions to all the problems. As the day wore on he could feel the blood pressure rising in his head. All of a sudden the information God had given me on the train was of infinite importance as a clue to why William suffers from this debilitating disease and why most of his life is lived inside a pressure cooker of work! The conversation ended with my asking him if he had enough courage to give every bit of himself and his life to God for God to deal with him as He saw fit. His answer was just 'Yes'.

The next morning was Sunday and we went to the Family Eucharist at the sixteenth-century All Saints church in Marlowe, just across a footbridge from our hotel. I will never be able to describe my feelings of joy and thankfulness for His unfathomable love for us all, that I felt that morning and ever since. About five minutes after our arrival a little old man came and sat beside us in our pew and said quietly, 'The wardens have decided to do things a bit differently today and instead of having a member of the regular congregation bring up the bread and wine at the Offertory, we think we'd like to have you and your husband do it today.' By this time the unexpected was almost the expected to me, but what a profound impression it made on William. The very giving of himself spiritually to God the night before was now being accomplished in the physical act of offertory with the elements. It was a moment filled with so much meaning for both of us!

In the afternoon we went on a tour of London and although I was with William and enjoyed that, I don't remember much of it. My thoughts were far away and still so sad until, all of a sudden into my mind came, 'Well, even if nobody really ever wanted me, God loves me and will make me into the person He wants me to be to do His work.' No sooner had that thought passed than all the answers to physical problems I've had during my life came to me. I have had a great deal of pain in the small joint at the base of my neck in front under my chin. Doctors and X-rays could never reveal what it was, because there was no evidence of fracture. But, Lucia, don't you remember how at my birth they twisted my head to try and turn me? They pulled my collar bone right out of joint. It was never set because it was never found and just grew improperly together all these years. A muscle in my back at my waist that has always very suddenly gone into spasm so that I can't move, was torn during the same twisting birth procedure. But since our time together at Whatcombe the most amazing things have happened. There has been an almost constant belching that continued for three whole days every three or four minutes. It seemed that all the colic air was still there, if that's possible, and finally came up. My stomach, which always protruded somewhat, has subsided and has never returned since!

Lucia, it seems that the experiences I've had in the last three months are meant to be shared and were not just for me. So, on returning home, I went to see our rector because the 'Barnabas Fellowship' seemed very relevant to my story and his spiritual counselling. After an hour of sharing everything with him, he praised God and thanked Him for these experiences. He said that God had brought them to him at a time of real crisis in his own ministry. He has felt all along that Agnes Sanford and others were correct: we must be healed of the past before our new life in Christ happens; how the 'death and resurrection cycle' must happen to each of us before we can even approach God's wishes and plan for our lives.

The impact of my story on the rector was so immense that he spoke of it (healing of the memories) in his Easter messages. Only God knows and will bring about the full meaning of what His wishes are for this type of ministry here, but I feel strongly that that is also part of the 'promise' of my work for God.

A week after returning home, William and I were sitting after lunch one day and he simply said, 'Ann, will you help God to help me remember why I'm the way I am?' And, Lucia, after praying with him, we lay down on our bed together and he poured it out – remembering horrible experiences of his father demanding jobs of work done, far too much for a small boy to do, struggling to do it quickly, but well, because he was afraid of his father's displeasure and working only for praise and a loving embrace that never came. The only goal in life seemed to be to please a father who was never completely satisfied and demanded only more of him. Then that changed, when he grew older, to 'I'll show him how worthy I am of his love.' He had to be first in everything, a perfectionist. He hated his younger brother who could do no wrong and was the 'apple of daddy's eye' and never lifted a hand at home. And then God showed us how the figure of father's authority changed to a boss's authority, and how he would work so hard to please a superior, while satisfaction (except salary increases) never was rewarded here, either. Only more work to do, with an ever-increasing role of responsibility.

But then, when we got down to the age of pre-natal life, the real miracle occurred – the fear changed from a fear of failure to a fear of death, and we couldn't get any further. I felt desperate. God had taken us so far and the only people who could help us were his parents now. I prayed so hard for guidance and the next day I went to see his parents. I explained, not in detail, what happened to me while visiting you and said that William had had a similar experience, but we were stopped at pre-natal life. I explained to them how William has two or three times a week for our whole marriage wakened from sleep, bolting out of bed, afraid and choking. They couldn't remember a thing for about half an hour and we had just relaxed over a coffee and I silently prayed that someone would remember something. All of a sudden his mother shouted out, 'Oh, my God, I remember. I remember!' During the first two months of pregnancy they had rented a cottage for the summer in an isolated and quite desolate area and during her first night there in the cottage she woke up simply terror-stricken that she was choking on the sheets of this unfamiliar bed, and tore screaming for breath out on to a small balcony. It lasted quite a long time and they eventually had to give up the cottage and come home to the city. The imprint of fear must have been so indelibly marked on William's psyche that he has been doing this same pattern of behaviour ever since. I'm sure you won't be surprised to hear it hasn't happened since he was told what had happened to his mother. Praise God!!

He really is like a different person, and when I asked him a couple of days ago how he felt inside he said, 'Ann, I'll never be afraid again as long as I live, because I'm never alone now!'

Our babes are relaxing and seem to be enjoying this new mummy and daddy that have just arrived on the scene, and I have prayed over them as you instructed me, Lucia. At Easter time my mother came to visit us for a few days and here is the final miracle story of this letter.

I felt moved to tell her one day what had happened to me at Whatcombe House, and said I felt that if she could listen to my story, her salvation was at the end of it, too.

She listened and cried bitterly as I had, and then she told me how she had been attacked and nearly raped by a thirty-year-old man when she was only thirteen years old. She spoke of her fear of men, her revulsion of their bodies, and how unworthy she felt of anybody's love. She said she was so afraid anything like that could happen to me, and she would have done everything to prevent it. Then she spoke of her own childhood, rejection and lack of love, leading her to believe that they didn't love her because she wasn't anything they could love – that she was worthless. So she built a wall round herself from being hurt anymore. No love could get in and no love could come out either – and so she lived out her tortured life. It even went so far as her relationship with God; she couldn't believe God could truly love someone like her and so she entered what she refers to as 'my spiritual desert', knowing God was available to others, but not to her. So, Lucia, we cried together, prayed together, and loved each other as real persons in the light of God's love.

This Easter has been the most beautiful and enriched time of all our lives, with the knowledge of the power of God right in our lives and homes. He loves us!!

My darling Lucia, who dared to put one hand in mine and your other hand in God's, to lead a whole family into the knowledge of Christ's love and gifts of salvation for all of us, I can never thank or repay you enough.

This letter has been quoted at length because it illustrates far better than I could describe certain lessons in the ministry of healing:

1. It demonstrates the 'chain reaction' of ministry. Having

ourselves been through the process of healing, we can be used, inexperienced as we may be, for the release of others. Our own release has shown the way that God will work.

2. It shows what can be done by someone who has a profound desire to see others free. Ann used the little she had and learnt that, when baffled, she could turn to God for help and guidance for the next step or for the knowledge she required for it to be taken.

3. Her story illustrates the importance of willingness to speak of God's action with ourselves. In doing this to her husband and mother she opened the way for both of them to pour out their own agony and need. Her mother's experience is common, as is that of her husband.

4. Her story is an illustration of the restoration of 'wholeness' which is the heart of healing: spirit, mind and body as a whole are healed by our Lord and as a whole person we receive a new beginning in Him.

12

The Spirit and emotional healing

Some have lost their attractiveness through suffering and our own resources are not sufficient to enable us to accept them without reserve. But the Spirit can cause compassion to well up and give such a consciousness of their distress that our reservations break down. The Spirit is able to lead us to sense their inner state as they themselves feel it. This leads to a relationship for a positive and radical ministry under the Holy Spirit.

Of the gifts of the Spirit, perhaps the most important for the healing of the past is the discerning of spirits. As we listen, we ask the Spirit to discern for us what are the essential factors. Often at the beginning of the conversation we feel inadequate and useless, and as the interview progresses the mass of detail can increase this sense. We therefore ask the Holy Spirit to indicate or discern for us the basic problems and pain areas. When baffled as to the cause we have to rely upon the Spirit to indicate what this is. Here is an example.

Katherine was a student nurse, attractive, open and friendly. She complained of being depressed, nervous and embarrassingly self-conscious. She had once suffered from nightmares which took the form of falling into a bottomless pit or of being lost. She walked in her sleep, usually fully dressing herself. Three years ago when she became a

Christian these night disturbances ceased. Now they had returned. She was in a highly nervous state, feeling confused and a failure and unable to think when with others. Now she could not eat with other nurses at table, being paralysed with fear, unable to pick up a knife or fork. She felt a failure as a Christian, condemning herself because she was not witnessing to Christ.

We found she was on night duty, but she enjoyed this and was on good terms with the ward sister. Her home life was not perfect, but she clearly loved her parents and was close to her mother. Her mother was a large woman of nineteen stone, of a nervous disposition, who feared going out, having a tendency to faint. Although mother could say to Katherine, 'If you are nervous, I have made you like that,' it did not seem that the home situation could alone be the cause of such trouble as Katherine was experiencing.

We felt lost, but as we were praying the thought came, 'Ask about Grandma.' We then found that when Katherine was small she was sent to Grannie's during her mother's two pregnancies. These were complicated and Katherine was away from home for a considerable time. Life at Grannie's was an unnerving experience. She gained her income by fostering children. Katherine believed that she did this, not for love of the children, but for financial gain. Grannie was a dominating, hard woman who struck fear into Katherine's heart. She had felt a terror which had never left her. One sensed something sinister as Katherine spoke. In that cold environment she was terrified, confused and lost. Back in her home this experience faded, but the damage was now having its effect.

We prayed through these years with Grannie and the Spirit gave us two texts which Katherine was to repeat to herself: 'Perfect love casts out fear' and 'The reason the Son of God appeared was to destroy the works of the devil.'

Shortly afterwards we had a letter: 'I don't have any problems now about eating in the dining room with the other nurses. The text you gave me to read, I John 3:8 has been a great help, giving me something to think about when otherwise I might have felt nervous. I've also noticed that I haven't been depressed or weighed down with problems, like I had been before.' The nightmares and sleepwalking had ceased.

In this instance the discernment was the Holy Spirit pointing us to the cause of the illness. At other times He will, as we listen, indicate the major influences and experiences we need to note. We would have arrived at Katherine's problem eventually through careful questioning, but as so often the Spirit indicated these things at the first interview. Though professional people may have the training to draw out the salient facts, one sees that the Spirit can give these to people who have had no psychiatric training. The Holy Spirit is able to use us remarkably through the gift of discernment, and the word of wisdom and the word of knowledge which are akin to it.

When the Spirit speaks we may hear actual words, but more often are aware of an impression – a thought comes to us strongly which fits the situation. We may be clearly led to ask certain questions or to explore an incident or period. The Spirit knows how best to signify to us His leading. We need have no concern about this. If we trust Him and concentrate on what the person is trying to express, He will direct us.

These gifts are valuable in those cases where people are not prepared to accept the basic cause of suffering. A man's emotional problem was his relationship with his father. The man denied this strongly at the first meeting and at the commencement of the second. However, as the Spirit continued to indicate the cause, questions were asked regarding the parent and it transpired that, out of fear, the man had spoken well of his father. In fact, he had lived in terror and hatred of him since a child, as had the whole family. He had never dared express what he really felt in case it should get back to his father. Having accepted the cause of his problems, he was released by our Lord from the fear and helped to make a new relationship with his father from an adult standpoint. But it was due to the Holy Spirit's pressure that we persisted in our examination of the parental relationship.

The Spirit lights up what we hear, makes us realise the importance of events, and leads us to an understanding of what really happened. When someone is in the centre of suffering it is almost impossible for him to see the situation clearly. As we listen, the Spirit will help us to see objectively and so we are able to show him a truer picture. One can often, for example, explain the problems of the parents and why they acted as they did. We are enabled by this gift to sense how people have themselves felt in particular experiences and how they feel as they speak of them to us in the present. This creates a fruitful relationship for ministry.

Other gifts from the list in 1 Cor.12 have been mentioned in chapter five and should not need further explanation. There is, however, an activity of the Spirit which frequently occurs when praying for the healing of the memories. This is the giving of visions or pictures. In this, a picture comes to one's mind. It may be a single picture or a continuing one. It is given to explain what is normally hidden. Such instances will occur when, in praying through the past, we are dealing with events before consciousness. When praying for the period when the foetus was in the womb, the Spirit has given visions. One was of a young woman sitting on a bed weeping and knitting agitatedly. This gave us an indication of the condition of the mother during pregnancy and was made more pertinent by the lady involved saying that her mother was a compulsive knitter.

On another occasion we were praying someone through a deep fear. We begged God to give us the source of it and He gave us a picture of a pram with a tiny baby. Beside the pram was a man in a great rage, arms waving and one foot raised to stamp. We then understood that such a frightening experience could have happened to her and that her fear was connected with her father. We then knew how we ought to pray.

Sometimes pictures are given to help the person realise their own emotional situation. One lady at a second interview said how God had given her three pictures. The first was that she was in a pit with railings around it. People were moving about outside but she could not get out. In the second she was in a paddock which had a wall round it. Jesus was on the other side of the wall. She ran to Him and said, 'I will pull down this wall.' He replied, 'No, I must do it.' The third was of a door tightly shut. Jesus said to her, 'This must open, but it will only do so slowly, and the light will come in a little at a time.' She, therefore, could realise her shut-in situation, that she could not free herself, but that Christ would open the way. She was, however, shut in tightly and the freeing would not be immediate. As we proceeded with the ministry all this proved to be true. Having had the pictures, she was able to co-operate because she could now see the situation which she had found difficult to understand.

These are ways in which 'the Spirit helps us in our weakness; for we do not know how to pray as we ought, but the Spirit himself intercedes for us with sighs too deep for words. And he who searches the hearts of men knows what is in the mind of the Spirit, because the Spirit intercedes for the saints according to the will of God' (Rom. 8:26–7). It is as we minister that we learn to be led by the Spirit and see the gifts operate. We should not concentrate on the gifts, but on the needs of the person. As we are taken up with this and lose awareness of ourselves, concentrating upon bringing God into the situation, the Spirit will act as and when He decides. We do, however, need to have an expectancy that He *is* actively engaged with us as we listen and pray. In this attitude of mind and heart, and as our sensitivity to the Spirit grows, we experience His activity.

As the problems of relationships, painful experiences and harmful emotions are prayed through and Christ heals, so the blockages are taken away. This, of course, is the outcome for which we are working and it should never be out of sight. The freeing from suffering – physical, emotional and spiritual – and the healing of relationships are a joy to see, but above all our life with God is paramount. After ministry, therefore, time has to be given helping a person to gain or regain oneness with God. Teaching about the spiritual life and prayer is necessary.

Reactions to ministry

How do people react under this prayer ministry? In no case has the writer found it has led to emotional disturbance. In fact, precisely the opposite has been the case, for it is the conflict of holding down intense emotions which produces problems. As our Lord releases these pent-up emotions the result is joy and peace.

With some little seems to happen outwardly. They come to an inner peace by the quiet realisation that they have been healed. Others feel nothing at the time, but gradually become aware that Christ has performed a healing. Such was a lady who was freed from her father's influence. He was a brutish man, hard and with a twisted sexual nature so that, she said, 'Even when he looked at his daughters we felt he was mentally undressing us.' He nevertheless had a love of the arts. After prayer it appeared that nothing had happened and for a month she was in a state of exhaustion. One day, looking in a shop window, she saw a picture which delighted her. She found herself saying, 'Oh! I wish father were here to see it,' and she realised that for the first time she was free of her fear and hatred of him.

A common reaction, both during speaking together and praying through the past, is to weep. Tears are often near to the surface. There may be quiet crying or deep sobbing. This is a release and it should be encouraged. Sobbing from the heart seems to have a beneficial effect in liberation.

At times someone will cry out things he has never before dared to admit, even to himself. 'I hate you! I hate you! I hate you!' is an example. One lady, as we were praying through her relationship with her mother, began to move her hands and arms as if strangling her mother. Later, when a serious scalding incident was being prayed through, she threw herself on the floor and screamed with the voice of a child of four or five. Some have rained blows at the wall with their hands and feet, others lying on the floor have hammered at it, shouting. One man's hands began to shake violently. 'It's in my hands,' he said, and a little later, 'Hold my hands.' As his hands were held, the shaking continued and he began to sob quietly. This ceased and he said, 'It's gone.'

It may be useful to end by quoting the impressions written by a young lady after receiving healing. She had had a most unhappy childhood and her marriage had failed. It is interesting that a scalding accident when a child and her marriage experience produced less reaction than other parts of her life. She had discussed her marriage difficulties with many people over a longish period and so there had been much emotional discharge. As regards the scalding, she remembered that she had screamed for a long time when the accident happened. We may compare her with the lady mentioned earlier who reacted strongly when her scalding accident was dealt with. Here is her account of what happened as we prayed.

I felt at the start of the interview that the help and love that I had already received through the fellowship of this house had healed and cleansed the wounds I was suffering as a result of the break-up of my marriage. As the interview progressed, I became aware that I had just been prepared for the experience of letting Jesus into my life. I realised that some calm had been achieved but the deeper, longer-term wounds were still there and very raw.

I will try to explain the emotions experienced but on many occasions they were more feelings of moods and colours than understandable and definable emotions.

On my conception I felt violation, rage, fear and hopelessness, not so exact but blackness and nothingness and fear.

The birth was very clear and again I felt my mother's outrage at the violation of her body, defiance, violence and hurt. Myself, I felt drawing back into the womb and the tightness and blackness of a hostile thing surrounding me. Total and awful fear as a tangible, touchable thing. The pelvis pressing down on me.

The scalding was a small nothingness, no fear, no sensation at all that I could define, a sort of shifting and moving grey colours.

The tonsils operation and growing fat I re-lived, I

didn't remember the feelings I had. I was again a frightened, unhappy, lonely child crying. The tears and sobbing out the misery that I couldn't and wouldn't do then.

The period from then until I met my husband was an extension of that feeling. I wasn't aware that I had suffered so much. All the little incidents were brought together and crystallised as one long, lonely, hopeless search for acceptance, love and companionship that I never found. I can't describe the true feelings, or explain the sobs. Perhaps the best explanation is of tight exploding groups of angry, hysterical colours. Black, blue, purple, red bursting in on each other with one despairing rageful twist and turn.

My marriage and my husband's hurt and bitterness were milder, almost expected continuations of this. Mixed with pity and awareness of the hopelessness and uselessness of the whole relationship from the start. I knew that there had never been a marriage in the true sense of the word, no coming together, no joining of minds or spirits.

Each emotion piled like a crescendo one upon another until I was battered down and helpless to control or direct the floods of feeling washing through and away from me.

I can write about this without any emotion except compassion and love. This person, these people (i.e. herself at different stages of life) who suffered are now dead and gone. A new person exists who is not connected with the old one except by pity for the hurt suffered.

The cutting from my Mother is still part of me. I can still feel the lurch of my whole inner being as the cord was cut. That sensation, I suppose of re-birth, is still with me. Nothing previously experienced compares with the physical wrench of being parted from my Mother.

I have just read what I have written and it seems a very lukewarm, pale description of the immensity that I experienced, but I know no way or words to get to the true heart of what I felt. The final cleansing and release, the calm, the quiet weariness, the readiness to take myself to God and say, 'Here I am. Please take me to You for all time,' is beyond explanation. Only someone who has experienced it and our Lord can understand that.

I am not the same person. I feel I should sign another name.

While this inner experience was going on, there was nothing happening outwardly. The lady sat quietly in the chair with little or no movement. Not everyone is able to articulate what they experience and many do not have such a strong reaction. Her account is given because she was able to write down the whole process and it provides an indication of what praying for the healing of the memories can achieve.

APPENDIX

The deliverance ministry

Cases do occur where the cause of distress is not emotional but demonic. In some denominations the relevant authority has given instructions regarding what action is to be taken. This should not be disregarded. Even so, Christians should have some knowledge of this subject so that they may act where no stipulation is made or when authority is given to proceed. Cases also occur where there is no time to go through 'normal procedure'.

Demonic action means that the powers of evil have enough influence upon a human personality to cause difficulty and suffering. If our attempts to free a person by dealing with emotional states produces little effect, or if, after some release, there is still distress, the possibility of evil spirits should be considered. A problem in this field is caused by some who appear to put all or most trouble down to Satan. This allows them to escape facing their own selves by passing the buck on to the Devil.

Nevertheless, the Devil is active and has to be taken into consideration. The Holy Spirit, by the gift of discernment, can alert us to the presence of evil spirits. There may be a sense of coldness, or of an evil presence or even smell. One may experience an inability to 'make contact' with the person concerned or there may be a feeling of revulsion. On one occasion, as a man was being prayed for, something emanated from him which resisted the blessing of God. As the evil presence was commanded to leave, the man shook and then came to peace physically and in spirit.

Apart from such indications by the Spirit, other factors may warn us of such evil activity. States of deep depression (sometimes alternating with happier periods) or of despair and lethargy could indicate such a possibility. The inability to read the Bible or to pray can be symptomatic and the inability to say the Name 'Jesus'. Compulsive desires for self-destruction or violence to others are likely pointers. A common cause is involvement with black or white magic, spiritualism, seances or ouija boards. Through such things evil powers can take hold, or because there may be family connections with such activities.

There may come from such sources spirit oppression or possession. The former means that there is external activity by evil presences. This usually results in depression or darkness being experienced for no apparent reason. Spirit possession (a questionable term) on the other hand signifies that in some way an evil spirit or spirits have entered and are active within the person. It seldom means that evil has taken control. Rather, if a spirit has obtained entry, the man will be aware of a force causing him to think and act in ways contrary to his normal behaviour.

As Christians we can have full confidence in Christ if we meet such evil activity. Our Lord is the power within us and He has given us authority over evil powers: 'The seventy returned with joy, saying, "Lord, even the demons are subject to us in your name!" And he said to them, "I saw Satan fall like lightning from heaven. Behold, I have given you authority to tread upon serpents and scorpions, and over all the power of the enemy; and nothing shall hurt you" ' (Luke 10:17–19). We should use this authority if we are in the presence of evil.

It is not wise to tell anyone that they are under the influence of evil spirits. It should come from them. For example, they may say during discussion that they or their family have been involved in ways mentioned earlier. The matter can then be gone into and should there be reasonable grounds for thinking they may not be free – especially if they themselves believe they are still affected by it – then action to deliver them should be taken. Influence of relatives, slight contact with seances or playing with ouija boards or glasses may cause only a 'contamination'. In such cases it is usually sufficient to drive the power away and pray for the mystical Blood of Jesus to cleanse and bring peace. The words, 'I command you in the Name of the Lord Jesus Christ to leave this child of God alone and I drive you from him,' will suffice. They can be told that if they sense any future oppression, they can deal with it similarly.

When someone tells us that he is possessed by an evil spirit, we need to question him as to why he should believe this to be so. As he tells us, we ask the Holy Spirit to signify if it really is the case. We proceed according to the leading. When we have no definite discernment or his reasons are insufficient, we assure him that the cause of his trouble is not satanic and proceed accordingly. If evil is present, action can be taken as described below, but we must first establish that he desires to be free and will receive Christ in place of the spirit. Unless we are assured of this, it is not prudent to go further. There are some, and an increasing number nowadays, who become involved with Satanism. This means a definite contract with the Devil and deep implication with evil. Such a person should be referred to someone who has had experience in this ministry.

To cast out an evil spirit, the following procedure may be used:

1. At least two people should be present with, if it can be arranged, the minister of the local church.

2. Protection is first claimed. This is to cover those present and others likely to be connected with them, such as members of their family. They should ask the Lord to cover them with the armour of God (Eph. 6:11), and with the protection of the Blood of Christ.

3. The evil spirit can then be bound with a command such as, 'Evil spirit I bind you in the name of the Lord Jesus Christ.'

4. The person involved must renounce any previous entanglement with evil or confess the sin that led to the spirit's entry, and also explicitly state his desire to be free from any involvement with evil powers and to ask that Christ should enter as Lord in place of the spirit.

5. The evil spirit is then cast out. A formula such as the following may be used, but there are traditional ones available for those who prefer to use them. 'Evil spirit, in the Name and by the authority and power given to me by the Lord Jesus Christ, I command you to leave this servant of God and never again to trouble him/her in any way.' Hands may be laid upon the person as those words are said. Some experienced in this ministry always consign the spirits to a place where they can do no further harm. They may, for example, be commanded to go into the hands of Christ.

6. After casting out, the person freed should take our Lord fully into himself, duly noting the warning given to us by Jesus (Luke 11:24–6).

A short bibliography

HEALING

Francis McNutt, *Healing* (Ave Maria Press).

Bernard Martin, *The Healing Ministry in the Church* (Lutterworth Press).

Agnes Sanford, *The Healing Light* (Arthur James). *Healing Gifts of the Spirit* (Arthur James).

Douglas Webster, *What is Spiritual Healing?* (Highway Press).

COUNSELLING

Ruth Fowke, *Coping with Crises* (Coverdale House).

Kathleen Heasman, *An Introduction to Pastoral Counselling* (Constable).

R. S. Lee, *Principles of Pastoral Counselling.* (S.P.C.K.).

Paul Tournier, *The Meaning of Persons, What's in a Name?* and other books (S.C.M. Press).

THE HOLY SPIRIT

Dennis and Rita Bennett, *The Holy Spirit and You* (Coverdale House).

John Gunstone, *Greater Things than These* (Faith Press).

Michael Harper, *Power for the Body of Christ* (Fountain Trust). *Walking in the Spirit* (Hodder and Stoughton).

John Rea (Ed.), *Layman's Commentary on the Holy Spirit* (Logos Publishing International).

GROUPS

John Gunstone, *The Charismatic Prayer Group* (Hodder and Stoughton).

THE DELIVERANCE MINISTRY

Michael Harper, *Spiritual Warfare* (Hodder and Stoughton).
Christopher Neil-Smith, *The Exorcist and the Possessed* (James Pike).
John Richards, *But Deliver us from Evil* (Darton, Longman and Todd).

TRAINING COURSES AND CONFERENCES ON COUNSELLING ARE ARRANGED BY THE FOLLOWING:

The Clinical Theology Association,
Lingdale,
Weston Avenue,
Mount Hooton Road,
Nottingham, NG7 4BA.

Victorious Ministry through Christ (GB),
c/o St. Luke's Vicarage,
Aylsham Road,
Norwich, NOR 1ON.

The Westminster Pastoral Foundation,
Matthew Parker Street,
London, S.W.1.

The Barnabas Fellowship,
Whatcombe House,
Winterborne Whitechurch,
Blandford, Dorset, DT11 0PB.

The Christian Renewal Centre,
Shore Road,
Rostrevor,
Co. Down, Northern Ireland.

Emily Gardiner Neal

THE HEALING POWER OF CHRIST

The continuing story of the healing Christ at work today, by a journalist who found Christ while seeking to 'expose' healing services, and subsequently developed a healing ministry of her own.

Here are many marvellous healings in the lives of men, women and children – sight restored after long-term blindness, the instantaneous disappearance of an abdominal tumour, a woman crippled with arthritis who, exhorted 'In the name of Jesus, walk!' straightened up, threw away her canes and walked.

'Of great value for sufferers and healers alike. This is something we have been waiting for . . . Based on a thorough study of Scripture and bears the authority of personal experience.' – *Marina Chavchavadze*

'*Rich material for the strengthening of one's own faith.*' – Baptist Times

'Deep spiritual understanding . . . offers hope and guidance to the perplexed and anxious.' – *Expository Times*

Ruth Carter Stapleton

THE GIFT OF INNER HEALING

'*These stories describing inner healing are the most moving and instructive examples on this subject I have ever seen.*' Francis McNutt, O.P.

Ruth Carter Stapleton, sister of Jimmy Carter, tells how she and others have been healed and helped to grow towards wholeness. By means of 'faith-imagination', she claims, one can, with the help of a concerned friend, know 'inner healing' or 'healing of the memories'. She writes:

'Since Jesus Christ is the same yesterday, today and tomorrow, he is able to go back into our lives and heal the traumatic episodes. He is the only one who can speak to our deepest needs and bring total healing to every person.'

'*Ruth Stapleton has a ministry of healing that has been of great benefit to many. Let us reap the insights that are given in her book and not attempt to be another Ruth.*' Colin Urquhart